LEG MAN
IN SEVEN-LEAGUE BOOTS

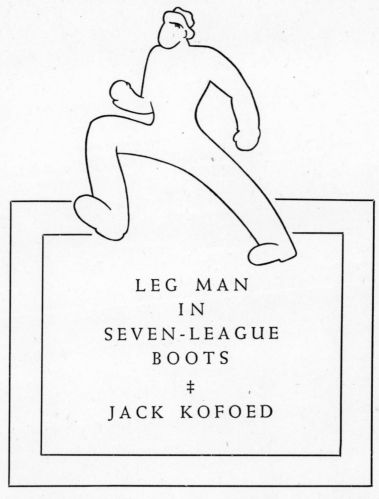

LEG MAN
IN
SEVEN-LEAGUE
BOOTS

‡

JACK KOFOED

ILLUSTRATED BY CRAWFORD PARKER
WITH AN INTRODUCTION BY EUSTACE L. ADAMS

GLADE HOUSE PUBLISHERS
CORAL GABLES, FLORIDA - 1946

This Book Is For

BILLY KOFOED

And his favorite soldier,

COL. T. J. J. CHRISTIAN

Also by Jack Kofoed

NIGHT CLUBS
[WITH JIMMIE DURANTE]

BEHIND THE GREEN LIGHTS
[WITH CAPT. CON WILLEMSE]

BRANDY FOR HEROES

THRILLS IN SPORTS

CONTENTS

INTRODUCTION

Dɪᴅ ʏᴏᴜ ever sit around for an evening with a grand guy who has been everywhere, seen everything and knows practically everybody — and he with a talking mood on him? First thing you know your heart grows warm when you find that you both used to hang around at Rector's and Reisenweber's, and the Cafe de la Paix and that place on Rue Blanche.

Well, that's this book. Jack Kofoed is a rare lad. His eyes grow misty when he talks and writes about the Good Old Days before the flea circuses took over 42nd Street, yet they light with enthusiasm over the things and the people he sees in this age of the Atomic Bomb and other assorted horrors.

Jack knows more celebrities than the desk clerks of the Astor, Roney-Plaza and Savoy combined. He loves them all. Or anyway, almost all. Maybe you won't love them — the princes and paupers, evangelists and gangsters — but you'll have a fine evening or two meeting them and seeing them through the eyes of a man who does.

Eustace L. Adams

PALM ISLAND
MIAMI BEACH, FLORIDA

I. THE TWIG IS BENT

*A small boy in Philadelphia
around the turn of the century.
The beginning of a leg man.*

I. THE TWIG IS BENT

I ALWAYS WANTED to meet interesting people. When I was a boy, living on Germantown Avenue in Philadelphia, it seemed I never would.

Not that the street itself lacked interest. Long and winding, its crooked length stretched from the Delaware River until it became lost in the remote suburbs of Chestnut Hill. There was historical significance to the thoroughfare. When it was only a country road, General Washington led his troops through its sun-flecked dust to victory over the British at Germantown.

But Washington and his men were gone with the dust, and Germantown Avenue had grown into shabby middle age. The part I knew—a limited segment between Lehigh and Indian Avenues—was lined on either side with stores protected by corrugated iron awnings, under which shoppers could stroll in comfort.

The street was paved with cobblestones, and wagon wheels made an unholy racket rumbling over them. The center of the avenue was preempted by a double row of trolley tracks; over those rods old fashioned, flat-wheeled cars trundled in noisy protest. Since the stores opened between seven and eight in the morning and did not close until nearly midnight, there was seldom a moment of quiet. One became used to the harsh symphony. People who moved to more peaceful neighborhoods found that stillness grated on their nerves. They missed the light and movement of Germantown Avenue.

Early of a winter morning yellow gas, or electric, lights blazed through the plate glass windows. On late summer evenings, when trade slackened, the storekeepers and their families moved chairs out on the sidewalk, but illumination still shone brightly in their shops. The owners of those stores were family men, and of no interest to a youngster who dreamed of adventure.

The only exception was my Dad. He sold shoes, but was not really part of any mercantile endeavor. He sailed the seas from the time he was twelve and ran away from a Danish home, until he became a master mariner and married mother; one of the iron men in wooden ships who made salt water history from the Indian Ocean to the Baltic.

According to my reckoning, Dad was the only one along the street who had accomplished anything. He talked little, but when he did, I saw Chinese sampans and heard the whistle of wind in the rigging as a ship floundered its way around the Horn. I caught glimpses of Marseilles and Copenhagen and Capetown. It seemed incredible that my father should be willing to stay on Germantown Avenue, and do the dull tasks required in a retail store. It was not until I was grown that I realized he had given up such a life for the love of my mother, who would not marry a roving seaman.

Nor were there any interesting characters in the back streets of our neighborhood. These people were laborers and mill workers, whose only relaxation was getting drunk on Saturday nights and turning their homes into bedlam. Their children went to school with broken shoes, holey stockings, and seldom had enough to eat. But their fathers bought cigars at Charlie Tag's tobacco store, and liquor at Hess' saloon, even when they could not pay rent or buy food.

The front of Tag's little store was piled to the ceiling with bales of tobacco. Its fragrance could be sniffed a block away, as could the Acme Tea Company because of the aroma of roasting coffee. Hess' was different. It was rank with stale beer, and that wasn't nice. But in the summer, by peeping under the swinging doors, the legs of men lined against the bar — feet resting on the brass rail — could be seen. They were familiar legs, and I could tell to whom they belonged, even though the doors were so high the faces weren't visible. The free lunch was tremendous . . . ham and cheese, dried fish, pickles and other thirst-inducing items. This was a masculine heaven, and because forbidden, it appeared bright and glamorous — but I never thought the men were.

At rare intervals one of Dad's cousins, a fat, florid sea captain named Emil Blem, came for a brief visit. He drank incredible amounts of *schnapps*, gorged on mother's bountiful food, and, except when eating, was never without a Holland cigar jutting from under his bushy mustache.

Captain Blem's freighter plied between Rotterdam and New York, with occasional trips to South America. His family lived in Copenhagen, but he had seen his wife and children only once in five years. Mother's refusal to endure such absences became understandable. The stout sailor was interesting only because of the places he had known, for Blem himself possessed no glamor. He talked with a thick, Scandanavian accent, and his breath was robust with memories of cheese and onions and brandy and tobacco.

There were nights when I went to the Reading Railroad yards and stood on the Huntingdon Street bridge. Whistling, roaring trains flowed under me. Engulfed in a cloud of steam, I pretended to be on those trains, traveling to marvelous places far away. Then I returned home, often through a flurry of snow. Home was warm and cozy, with a turkey-red cloth on the dining room table, and an ice box crammed with good things to eat. Under the gas light, Dad kept company with a glass of beer and a sandwich, while Mother hustled about, completing her last chores before bedtime.

Dull, proletarian, uninteresting. That's the way it seemed, though I had no such words in my vocabulary. A thousand times since I have thought of those days and nights. I have thought of them at the front, under bombings; in swank night clubs; in conversation with important people of the world. Softened by the patina of time, they seem good. But I know they were not interesting, and would not be if I had to live them again.

There were a few contacts with excitement. One of the first movie companies, Lubin, owned a studio on Indiana Avenue, only a few blocks from my home. The stars of their primitive flickers were Florence Lawrence and Harry Myers. Memory plays tricks, but still it seems that even Lana Turner and Betty Grable lack the fascinating beauty of Miss Lawrence. Scenes were shot in streets adjacent to the studio, and I spent breathless moments watching my first romantic heart-throb going through what were generously known as histrionics.

But Harry Myers, the Clark Gable of his day, left me quite cold. His collar was too high, his pants too tight, and it seemed silly for a grown man to paint his face. Besides, Harry lived on Willington Street, and could be seen around the neighborhood after working hours, when he was not in the least romantic.

In addition, on the perimeter of my Germantown Avenue existence, was the Philadelphia National League baseball park at Broad Street and Lehigh Avenue. Baseball was one of the most important facts of life. The Phillies were heroes and all other teams villains in each six months cyclorama of feuding.

The New York Giants, in particular, earned our undying hatred. When they visited Philadelphia, they lived at the Majestic Hotel, and, fully uniformed, were driven to the ball park in a horse-drawn bus. We youngsters stood on the street corner and screamed maledictions at such national heroes as John McGraw, Christy Mathewson, and "Iron Man Joe" McGinnity. If there were no policemen at hand, we'd supplement the verbal barrage with another of rotten tomatoes. Never since have I known such honest, boiling hate.

On the opposite side of Broad Street, catercornered from the ball park, stood an old hotel called the Junction House. Most of the Phillies lived there because it was cheap and convenient. Generally speaking, they were rough young men, with no pretension to education or the social graces, but in my unsophisticated judgment they were demi-gods.

I watched them play from a heat-blistered twenty-five cent seat in the bleachers. In the evening I strolled past the Junction House. The heroes were sprawled in chairs ranged in front of the hotel, chewing tobacco, gossiping, whistling at the girls. Strangely enough, while the actor, Harry Myers, lost stature in his own neighborhood, I felt a kinship with greatness when coming close to these ball players in their hours of ease.

My favorite player was a dour, taciturn outfielder named "Silent John" Titus. He had come from a Pennsylvania farm to the big league diamonds, but had never adopted urban ways. In the hottest weather, John wore a heavy broadcloth suit with a gold watch chain draped across the vest. His only recreation was burlesque shows. Night after night he occupied a gallery seat at the Gaiety, Trocadero or Bijou theatres, but was never seen at stage doors seeking dates with the chorus girls. When the curtain fell on the last shabby scene and final dubious joke, Titus returned to the Junction House for a night of righteous sleep.

All baseball players are superstitious. By devious ways, I learned that "Silent John's" fetish was women's hair pins. He firmly believed that for each one he found on the short walk from the hotel to the ball park, he would get a hit that day. I could not quite see the connection, but I wanted to help him. I stole a few hair pins from mother's dresser and loafed about the Junction House until John's broadclothed and impressive frame appeared in the doorway. Then I strolled ahead of him and surreptitiously dropped two or three pins. The plan worked. Titus went on an extended hitting spree — but mother soon caught me pilfering her pins.

These contacts with the only important people I knew were not enough. I had never said more than "Hi!" to Titus, or Charlie Dooin, or "Fiddler" Sparks, and had never ventured even that far with gorgeous Florence Lawrence. Of course, the theaters brought great public idols into view. Edwin Booth, Edna May and Dan Daley starred at the Walnut Street Theater. The South Broad's musty walls held memories of John Drew, Nat Goodwin, Maude Adams, Lillian Russell and DeWolfe Hopper. The Chestnut Street Opera House resounded with applause for Henry Irving and Ellen Terry. No one less than Victor Herbert led the orchestra. But these people were to be seen only from the long range of the gallery. They were vague and remote. I did not get close to them, but they strengthened my determination to meet and know interesting people.

Each summer my brother, Will, and I spent a month with a cousin who lived near Fort Hamilton in Brooklyn. The house was only a short ride from Coney Island, and to me the Island was the brightest, gayest, liveliest place in the world. After a morning on the beach, there was lunch at Joe's, where a dime purchased a huge bowl of steaming clam chowder and all the bread and butter we could stuff.

There were Luna Park and Steeplechase, fairylands of lights and thrills. And I began to learn something of what are called the "facts of life" on Coney Island's Bowery.

It was redolent with the smells of hot dogs and buttered corn and beer. There were noisy barkers in front of every saloon that featured entertainment. In several of these places were mezzanines, each with a dozen cubicles. From these, scantily clothed women signalled potential customers on the main floor. The sidewalks were crowded with prostitutes who solicited openly. Unless they became drunk and disorderly, the police never interfered. There were strange men who painted their faces and used exaggerated feminine gestures. It was something new, and not entirely understandable. A shoddy part of life I had never dreamed of. But it was interesting.

The closest I had come to the fringes of the underworld was an occasional walk in Philadelphia's Tenderloin. I remember Jerry Donahue's saloon at Eighth and Vine Street, which had a square bar and John L. Sullivan's diamond belt on exhibition. I remember the peanut and shine boys on Eighth Street; picture houses, where you dropped a penny in a machine and turned the crank; Chinatown around the corner, which was Canton in a small way, where a lovely dinner could be bought for thirty cents. But I had never seen anything like the Bowery at Coney Island.

It was in 1910 that stark and brutal drama came within my ken.

The motormen and conductors of the Philadelphia

Transit Company went on strike. Some left their trolley cars on the tracks and walked away. Hoodlums pushed those cars on their sides, and set them on fire. The pulse of the city began to beat faster. Trouble was sensed in the air. Trolleys were manned by strike breakers and guarded by police. They made only token runs, for passengers were afraid to board them. One came clattering at top speed north on Germantown Avenue, its bell clanging furiously, never slowing for an instant at intersections. A policeman, wearing the high helmet of the era, stood on the platform beside the motorman. In the block between Lehigh Avenue and Somerset Street the car and its crew were showered with rocks and bricks.

The second day the attackers tired of long range gunning, and upended a city trash wagon across the tracks. It made a solid road block. The motorman of the next trolley to come along had no choice but to grind on his brakes, even though he knew that, once stopped, he was a lost soul. The policeman unholstered his gun, and tried to protect his charge, but had no chance. He was brushed aside, and rioters dragged the strike breaker into the street.

The man was middle aged, with greying hair and a walrus mustache. He tried to explain that his family was hungry, but the rioters wouldn't listen to him, and ripped off his clothes. When I last saw him he was running up Germantown Avenue clad in long, greyish underwear. His face was bloody, and sort of pulpy. The sight made me sick at my stomach.

The police decided stronger methods were necessary.

21

They sent in foot and mounted details, and Germantown Avenue became a saturnalia of violence. Probably because they were nervous, the blue coats took the offensive and beat up men and women indiscriminately. Gashed heads, broken noses and blackened eyes became common sights in what had been a peaceful neighborhood. This added fuel to the fire. Even folk who had taken no part in earlier brawlings resented these methods and joined in rioting.

The police admitted defeat by asking that the State Fencibles, as the Pennsylvania militia was called, be ordered into action. This was done, but the newspapers announced that the amateur soldiers were on guard with unloaded rifles. What followed was a sin and a shame. Mobs took the guns away from the Fencibles and chased them from their posts. There was only one remaining thing to do: summon the Pennsylvania State Police.

They were a combination of Texas Ranger and Northwest Mounted, who were known as "Black Cossacks" to the coal miners of the Keystone State, whose strikes they had helped break. They were hard men, trained and disciplined in handling trouble. The first one to appear on Germantown Avenue rode his horse almost casually down the street. His uniform and helmet were black. He carried two holstered pistols, a shotgun and riot stick in saddle scabbards. But it was not his armament that impressed the people. It was the reputation of the State Police, and his cold, competent manner. Even the tough boys of the back streets shrank from his glance. The crowds shredded out and went their way. This happened wherever the troopers appeared. The strike, and attendant riots, died on the vine. Germantown Avenue resumed its tranquil ways.

One thing I learned from Florence Lawrence and "Silent John" Titus and the Pennsylvania State Trooper, whose name I never knew, was the importance of knowing one's job. They all knew theirs: Titus in handling a ball and bat, Miss Lawrence in portraying emotions before a camera, the cold-eyed state trooper in quelling trouble. They had confidence in their ability to use the tools of their trade. That's why they succeeded. I decided to remember that.

II. THE FIRST STEP

*Odyssey of a newspaperman and
some of the people met enroute:
good, bad and indifferent.*

II. THE FIRST STEP

I WANTED TO BE a newspaperman and go places and see people. There were a good many papers in Philadelphia, *The Public Ledger, Bulletin, Inquirer,*

Record, Press and *Telegraph* among them. Though I had no knowledge of the business, and no acquaintanceship among its editors, I made an appearance in the city rooms nearly every day. A young beggar, hat in hand, "A job, please, sir, any kind of job!" Refusals were unanimous at first, but I kept going back.

Everyone in newspaper offices seemed important to me. Ageing men wearing eyeshades, on the rim of the copy desk; rewrite men, listening over telephones; the brisk city editor; all were part of a world I wanted to make mine.

Probably because it was easier to give me a job than to keep refusing, I found myself in this enchanting business. Mother didn't like the idea. She believed all newspapermen were loose morally and drank too much. But there I was.

The first important and interesting man I saw in action was Philadelphia's ace criminal lawyer, John R. K. Scott. He was the Bill Fallon of the Quaker City's legal jungles, and possessed, among other things, a vast estate: butlers, foxhounds and automobiles.

I was assigned occasionally to Criminal Court. On one occasion Mr. Scott was defending a man accused of rape. The noted counsellor seemed to doze fitfully through the prosecution's testimony. This, to an amateur like myself, seemed proof of his client's guilt.

But then Scott rose to address the jury. He made no impassioned plea. He simply brought out a target rifle, and thrust the barrel toward the jury foreman.

"Stick your finger in it," he ordered.

The foreman tried, but the lawyer jerked the gun aside, and the foreman's digit missed the aperture.

"I can't put it in if you pull it away," he protested.

"Exactly," said Mr. Scott sardonically. He followed this procedure with the other eleven men, tried and true. They all failed. "Gentlemen, I rest my case," he said.

His client was acquitted.

This seemed to me almost as clever and capable as the feat of Jack Coombs, the Athletics' great right-handed pitcher, who struck out three men in a row with the bases loaded.

Sports were my hobby and I followed them avidly. Charlie Dryden, Ring Lardner, Bob Maxwell, Heywood Broun, James C. Isaminger, Sam Crane, Bill McGehan, Grantland Rice were my idols and my pattern. They lifted sports writing into a specialized and highly paid phase of newspaper work. I wanted to be like them.

After the first World War, and a year and a half in France, I joined the sports department of the *Evening Ledger*. The sports editor was Bob "Tiny" Maxwell, a fabulous personality, who weighed 320 pounds, and wore an automobile tire inner tube to hold up his sagging abdomen. He was one of the kindest, wittiest and most understanding men I've ever known. Bob had been an All-American football player and for years was one of the best gridiron officials.

He once handled a game between Holy Cross and Boston College. Contests between Catholic institutions are notoriously rough, but this one was a riot. It was climaxed when a Boston end tackled a Holy Cross back, and sank his teeth into the unfortunate ball carrier's leg. Tiny had overlooked many infractions of the rules so that the contest might not be slowed by excessive penalties. This, however, was too much.

Maxwell waved an admonitory finger.

"Listen, you harp," he roared. "This is Friday. No meat on Friday, you understand, no meat at all!"

Strangely enough, it was a tragedy that gave me my first opportunity to become a columnist. Tiny owned a 12-cylindered red Packard sports roadster, which was the talk of Philadelphia. He also had a cottage in Betzwood, where he staged gala week-end parties.

Coming back from one of these affairs, roaring through the night at sixty miles an hour, Maxwell's Packard smashed into a truck. His ribs caved in, puncturing his lungs. It was a shock to us at the paper, because we all loved the man. Some of us went to see him in the hospital the next afternoon. His round, good-humored face was grey with pain. We stood around restlessly, not knowing what to say.

"Look, Doc," said Tiny. "Don't kid me. When am I due to check out?"

"You haven't got more than a couple of hours," answered the man of medicine unhappily.

Maxwell grinned at us. "Don't make a funeral out of this," he said. "Doc, get a couple of bottles of champagne. I might as well kick-in with a laugh."

We drank with him, and he died an hour after we left. He was a fine and brave gentleman to the last.

Maxwell had been the columnist, as well as sports editor, of the *Evening Ledger*. His passing created a vacancy. It was one I hoped to fill. Members of the staff took turns occupying the space our boss had handled so competently, but none of us was handed the assignment. Management usually sees greener grass in other pastures, and Stoney McLinn was brought in from Chicago.

However, I was given a column in the *Public Ledger*, the asthmatic and financially incompetent step-child of the *Evening Ledger*. It wasn't what I had wanted, but it was a rung up the ladder. My work caught the eye of Frank Walker, who was publishing the New York *Telegram* for the universally-hated Frank Munsey. Mr. Walker asked me to replace James Kevin McGuinness, who was leaving to become an immensely successful Hollywood motion picture producer.

Munsey was a groceryman, who made millions at everything he touched. He owned, among other things, newspapers and magazines, about which, in an editorial sense, he knew nothing.

There probably was never a harder hearted man in the newspaper business than Munsey, with the single exception of Charles Chapin, the sadistic city editor of the New York *World*. When Chapin planned to discharge a reporter or desk man, he saved the event for a day which should have been a happy one for the victim . . . Christmas Eve, perhaps, or a birthday, or wedding anniversary. It made the loss of a job more poignant, and Chapin proportionately happier.

Well, I ran into trouble at the start on the *Telegram*. Mr. Walker wouldn't give me a by-line.

"Hell's bells!" I protested, "that's my stock in trade. Why don't you want to let me profit by it?"

"Because," Walker said pontifically, "if you do as good a job as I expect you to, other papers will make offers, and then we'll have to pay more money, or lose you."

"That," I told him, "is the lousiest argument I ever heard." But Walker wouldn't change his mind. So I stayed with the *Telegram* for six months working under Nat Fleischer, an old hand at the business. It was a sort of enchanted mesa to me. I was disturbed at not having a by-line on the column, but that was the only cloud on the horizon.

Then, white-bearded old Cyrus H. K. Curtis bought the New York *Evening Post*, which for one hundred years had been a financial white elephant. Under his ownership it became the most colossal money-loser in newspaper history.

Curtis named G. Merritt Bond, who had been managing editor of the *Ledger*, as the man to lift the pathetic 28,000 circulation of the *Post* to a respectable level. Bond offered me a job, I accepted and stayed for ten years. The *Post* never did get much beyond the 100,000 mark in sales, and Curtis poured millions into it. When he died, his heirs did not want any part of the paper, and it passed into other hands. I went on to William Randolph Hearst's *Journal*.

I got to know New York . . . its people and its component parts. I saw the city at all hours of the day and night. Dawn in the Fulton fish market. The cocktail hour in Park Avenue penthouses. Ball games at the Yankee Stadium and Polo Grounds. Prize-fights at Madison Square Garden. Night court, where the dregs of the city were sentenced for their sins.

I began to meet interesting people; all sorts. Theodore Drieser, the novelist. Ray Long, the most famous magazine editor in the world, and his executive editor, William C. Lengel. Tex Rickard, Jack Dempsey and Babe Ruth. Mayor Jimmy Walker, who admitted he was never at his best until after midnight. Al Smith, with his brown derby and grating pronunciations. Johnny Broderick, the toughest detective in New York. Jimmy Durante, Eddie Cantor and Phil Baker. Ministers and business executives. Prostitutes and speakeasy owners. John Edgar Hoover, Dutch Schultz and Owney Madden. Theatrical producers and chorus girls. Stevedores and housewives and the old and forgotten people of the East Side tenement.

I learned that the best stories do not always come from important people, and success has nothing to do with interesting personalities. Some of the most exciting characters never achieved much materially, and had no desire to do so; while some of the most famous ones turned out to be quite dull.

People are the steel, concrete and mortar from which columns are built. Fundamentally they are the same, whether their habitat is New York or Kenosha, Wisconsin.

III. LEG MEN

*Men who make a newspaper.
The personalities behind the
by-lines, giants of journalism.*

III. LEG MEN

TAKEN BY AND LARGE, newspapermen are as literate, well-informed and presentable as any specialized group in the world. Their ethics do not suffer in comparison with those of the law, medicine or the church. Few betray confidences or their source of information.

But newspapermen probably pan their profession more than any other example of genus homo. They invent ribald jokes about the game, and insist they would strangle their babies at birth if they had any idea printers' ink sullied the infant blood. This is no more than pretense in most cases. It's a fine trade, always creative, and sometimes exciting. It was once considered humorous to tell friends: "Don't tell my mother I'm a newspaperman. She thinks I play piano in a whore-house."

The movies have helped build an entirely erroneous impression about the ladies and gentlemen of the Fourth Estate. There are a few types that never seem to die on the silver screen . . . the cub reporter, who scores a terrific scoop and marries the boss' daughter; the drunken news-hawk; the irascible city or managing editor, who continually misses getting married because a story pops up just when he is about to march to the altar. These are ninety per cent the inventions of moronic minds.

In the first place, newsgathering is such an organized business that a cub has as much chance to scoop the world as he would to empty Biscayne Bay with a teaspoon. In the second place, a drunken reporter will find himself out of a job permanently. In the third, if a newspaper is so loosely organized that a city or managing editor can't take time off to get married, it's a cinch the rag would soon go into bankruptcy. The newspapermen you see portrayed in the movies are not the newspapermen who bring you the daily record of the world happenings.

There's another point that needs a bit of clearing up. Most people think that members of the Fourth Estate are as poorly paid as Bob Cratchit. When I was sports editor of the New York *Evening Post*, I ran into a friend whom I hadn't seen for a number of years. He was an executive of a big coal company, and had under his immediate supervision some eight or ten heating engineers.

My friend deplored the fact that I had edged into a business that was the worst paid on earth. That needled me a little.

"Let's pass up for a moment," I said, "the publishers, who have made millions. Let's even pass by such people as Heywood Broun, Damon Runyon, Walter Winchell and others of similar standing, whose pay ranges from $50,000 to $250,000 a year. Let's just look at the average guy. What do your engineers make?"

Well, it seemed their average salary check was $45 a week, with a top of $75 for the senior.

"And you think newspapermen have to go around with tin cups, do you?" I asked. "I have eleven men in my department. Four of them get $90 a week and the average for the entire staff is a little better than $70." There was nothing for my friend to do but admit he had been slightly off when it came to the matter of paychecks.

A good many fine writers have deserted their first love for the movies, the theater, magazine writing, advertising and publicity, but they were not exactly poverty stricken when they made the change. I have never known any who did not suffer nostalgic twinges when thinking of deadlines and printers' ink and such things.

One of the first to head for Hollywood was James Kevin McGuinnes, whom I succeeded as sports columnist of the *Telegram*. McGuinness showed me a contract for $30,000 a year as a "title writer," the trade name for dialogue moulders in the silent pictures in 1924. Since then his income has risen to five or six times that amount.

Another renegade was "Red" Nolan, who never became famous, but as a good journeyman worked in the film capital for many years. Red lived frugally in a small house, used a battered Ford to carry him about and never attended parties. He didn't like Hollywood, or the people in the picture business, and when he had accumulated $100,000, he quit the business with a sigh of relief.

Nunnally Johnson and Dudley Nichols were members of the staff of the New York *Evening Post* when I moved there from the *Telegram*, but they headed West and are now among the most intelligent producers in Hollywood. Their incomes are fabulous, certainly far beyond anything they could have earned in newspaper work, even if they had owned papers instead of reporting for them. But, as has been said before, money isn't everything.

One of the most illustrious deserters from the Fourth Estate was Gene Fowler, a man of writing talent and ribald imagination. In his Fire Island hideout, Fowler wrote such best sellers as "The Great Mouthpiece," "Shoe the Wild Mare," "Timberline" and "Goodnight, Sweet Prince." Between times, he condescended to pen occasional movie scenarios at fees ranging from $50,000 to $100,000.

Those of us who were working newspapermen, and remained as such, remember Gene not only as a great reporter, but a master at hoaxing an expense account. It is recorded that a Hearst city editor once refused to send him to Jersey City to cover a tremendous fire.

"The God damned fool," remarked the city editor, "will charter a ferry boat to get him there, and the story isn't worth that much to us."

When Fowler, in one of the perennial Hearst shakeups, was named managing editor of the New York *American* he became hated by every reporter on the staff. Since Gene knew all the tricks, the wisest of expense account chiselers could edge nothing past him.

What was originally known as the Broadway . . . and is now generally called the gossip . . . column, came into faint and labored birth through S. Jay Kaufman, of the New York *Telegram*. Kaufman apparently had no idea of its tremendous potential. Either that, or he lacked the temperament to carry through to the inevitable conclusion. At any rate, it was not until a sharp-featured, ex-vaudeville hoofer took up a stint on what was probably the worst newspaper ever printed—the New York *Graphic*—that the gossip column came into its own. This was the debut of Walter Winchell, with his insatiable curiosity, incredible vitality, and almost shocking flair for coining words and phrases, like "middle-aisling" for marriage and "renovate" for divorce.

Winchell's rise in the newspaper firmament was probably the most spectacular of all time. It was bound to be, for he had struck, if not a new note, certainly an utterly unique rendition of it, in the newspaper symphony. It became a stock gag that no woman who thought herself with child could be sure unless she first asked the omniscient W. W. if it were true.

In 1933 I found I was about to become a father for the second time. My wife and I decided we could keep it a secret until, in a physical sense, it could no longer be hidden. But one Monday morning, a line appeared in Walter Winchell's column: "The Jack Kofoed's are infanticipating."

This was a miracle. It simply couldn't happen. There had been no intimations of witchcraft in America since the Salem burning, but what was this? I pinned Walter in a corner of the Stork Club and demanded an answer to the mystery. He countered with the oldie all of us in the craft know by heart: "I never divulge the source of my information."

Eventually I found out. The only person I had informed as to the coming of a second heir was an old friend named Charles Dexter, who was currently laboring as a writer in the well-paid galleys of Hollywood. Since Dexter was three thousand miles away, it seemed the secret was as safe as a show bet on Man o' War in a two horse race. But Charles had hustled to a Western Union office and telegraphed the news to Winchell!

This detracted nothing from the magic. At the start

Walter hand-spaded news himself. In a short time he became an oracle. People like my cinema friend volunteered to aid him. It is a gift of the gods to wangle such support.

Naturally, such a lush field could not be hoed by a single man. Others followed with variants of the original pattern: Ed Sullivan, Danton Walker, Earl Wilson, Leonard Lyons, Dorothy Kilgallon, Sidney Skolsky and Louis Sobol, among others.

Each was taken not only to the heart of New York, but, through syndication, to the heart of America. Their incomes make many a bank president envious.

In newspaperwork, as in medicine or surgery, specialization is the highroad to success. O. O. McIntyre's column was the most widely syndicated of his day. It recorded the current history of New York through the eyes of a small town man. This was sheer theater on McIntyre's part. Though he pretended, for the benefit of his readers, to jibe at the opulence and fandangoes of Manhattan, no one wallowed deeper in them than he.

I once stopped at Odd's incredible penthouse to accompany him to a Dutch Treat Club dinner at the Waldorf. The hotel was only a few blocks away and the evening was lovely. McIntyre, decked in the only purple evening clothes I have ever seen, insisted on being driven there in his Rolls Royce, equipped with chauffeur and footman. The gaping observers on the sidewalk must see him descend from his barouche. His small town complex was strictly for reader consumption. No one typified the sybaritic side of New York more exactly than O. O. McIntyre.

Half a century ago sports writing was an extra duty assignment for some desk man with a few leisure moments. But it came into its own as a well-paid specialty long before the gossip column was born. From the sports department have come such noted writers as Damon Runyon, John Kieran, Quentin Reynolds, Paul Gallico, Westbrook Pegler and Ring Lardner.

Arthur Brisbane called Runyon the greatest reporter that ever lived and he was not far off in his estimate. Damon is also a fine columnist, and an extraordinary short story writer, who has translated the language of Broadway to the printed page as no one else has ever been able to do.

Runyon, for all his success, is a modest man. I happened into his apartment in the Parc Vendome when the success of the motion picture, "Lady for a Day," brought a score of telegrams offering him up to $25,000 each for the right of other yarns he had written.

"I'm not kidding myself," Damon said. "This is just a vogue. It won't last. I'm going to stash this money away, because there won't be much more like it." But he wasn't a passing vogue. Runyon is as popular as ever. Amazingly, he is extremely well-liked in England, where it would seem his purely localized slang would miss the mark completely.

There's a funny story connected with "Lady for a Day." A producer at Columbia Pictures was convinced it would make a great picture, and persuaded Prexy Harry

Cohn to pay $5,000 for it. Cohn went to Europe, and when he came back, found that "Lady" ranked with "It Happened One Night" as one of the most sensational films Columbia had ever made.

Harry thumbed through a collection of Runyon short stories, and indicated one. "We'll make that one next," he commanded.

"But, Mr. Cohn," said the producer, "we don't own the rights to any of those."

"What?" yelled the tycoon. "We paid $5,000 for one story? I thought it was for the whole book."

The part of America which didn't know John Kieran as a sports commentator, has come to know him as an infallible expert on everything. Kieran is certainly the most erudite person who ever made his living writing sports. He reads omnivorously, and his photographic memory enables him to retain what he reads. Whether it is the habits of an obscure tropical bird, a quotation from Shakespeare, or the score of a baseball game played in 1905, John Kieran is seldom in error.

Westbrook Pegler has made a greater reputation attacking labor unions and the Democratic administration than he ever did accusing prize-fighters of crookedness in the ring, and he did that frequently as a sports writer. He is utterly fearless, but has a soured and unhappy view of humanity. As one of his co-workers once remarked: "Peg doesn't even believe the Crucifixion was on the level!"

Pegler has neither Winchell's nor Runyon's flair for phrase making, but one remark credited to him is a classic.

He was covering a golf tournament for International News Service years ago. The gallery huddled around the green watching Walter Hagen putt. Peg, like the other reporters, half knelt before them, taking notes. Someone behind him said, "Get down lower, will you?"

Without turning, the sports writer answered, "I work for Hearst. I can't get any lower than that!"

Pegler was, however, absolutely honest. When it became known that Tex Rickard, the fight promoter, had some New York sports writers on his payroll, Westbrook was never one who came under suspicion.

"There's one reason I wouldn't take anything from Tex," he said. "If, while strolling with my wife, I met Rickard, I wouldn't want him to be able to say to himself, 'I bought that dress Mrs. Pegler is wearing.' " There were a dozen other reasons, too, but this was enough.

Runyon, Pegler, Ring Lardner—as complete a master of the short story as Runyon—and Paul Gallico, who is only a hitch behind them in that art, all quit sports writing for wider fields. So did the vast and sloppy Heywood Broun, perhaps the best loved of all columnists. One of the most pleasant memories of my life is the time spent working with that lovable tilter-at-windmills on a radio program called "The Magazine of the Air."

Broun had a magic touch with words. When he covered a World Series baseball game in which Babe Ruth was the hero, he wrote: "The Ruth is mighty, and must prevail," and beyond that I cannot go. His big heart and sense of humor allowed him to combine a "Daily Worker" viewpoint with "New Yorker" phrasing, and still work for the capitalist press.

There are many, though, who stuck to writing sports, and wanted nothing else. Grantland Rice, Dan Parker, Joe Williams, Bill Cunningham and Bill Corum, found the passing parade from Dempsey to Louis, Cobb to Ferris, Hagen to Nelson, filled their emotional vacuum as completely as it did their pocketbooks. So, too, did Hype Igoe, Sid Mercer, Frank Graham, Ed Bang, Ed Pollock and countless more. They lifted sports writing from an unenviable chore to one of the most important assignments on a newspaper.

In recent years the war correspondent has stolen the thunder and the headlines from all other reporters of doings in an uneasy world. His may seem a glamorous task to the casual reader, but it is filled with danger, effort and the annoyances of military censorship. No war has ever been covered as thoroughly, intelligently and courageously as this one just past. And, in the covering, some men who had not been particularly conspicuous at their trade gained sudden stature.

Ernie Pyle, who had worked on the copy desk of the New York *Post;* Quentin Reynolds, a sports writer for the New York *World;* Jack Bell, former sports editor of the Miami *Herald;* are perhaps the outstanding examples.

Pyle was as small town in heart and mind as O. O. McIntyre was in pretense. Frail and sickly, he endured all the hardships of the GIs in many a campaign before a

Japanese bullet killed him on the Ie Jima beachhead. His courage was magnificent. The hunch that he would not live through the Normandy invasion plagued him, but he went over with the shock troops just the same. He felt the same proddings about the Pacific campaign, and they turned out to be true.

Jack Bell, who had lost an arm as a machine-gunner in the first World War, was also cut from the Pyle pattern. His primary interest was the little man; the dogface who lived and died in the mud.

Reynolds, an ex-sports writer, came into a war correspondent's uniform almost accidentally. As a staff member of *Collier's*, his stories about baseball players and prizefighters had grown flat and dull. His interest was gone, and his touch with it.

Then Frank Gervasi returned from a tour of duty overseas. Gervasi was weary to the bones and needed a rest. His suggestion that Quentin replace him in London was received coldly at first, for the powers that be were convinced that Reynolds had outlived his usefulness. But Gervasi was persuasive . . . and under the bombs that showered down on the British capital, the sports writing Stork Club habitue wrote some of the most moving stories of the war.

One of the aristocracy of the newspaper world . . . if success and money predicate such aristocracy . . . was Arthur Brisbane, who was William Randolph Hearst's chief factotum for many years. Brisbane laid down the law of the Medes and the Persians in his first page column, as well as dictating the editorial policy of a score of papers.

I sat beside that gentleman in the press row at the Tommy Loughran - Primo Carnera fight in Florida one night. He was accompanied by a prominent society woman. The lady was impressed by Carnera's immense size, and voiced her wish to bet on him.

A gambler behind her offered to accept the wager, and she matched his two hundred dollars. Thereafter the damsel cheered Primo, and shouted for him to knock Loughran's block off. It was a natural reaction, since her money was on the line. Even Mr. Brisbane shaved some of his glacial manner, and indulged in a few faint hurrahs.

However, in his next day's column he mentioned, as he had been doing for years, that a gorilla could have beaten both of the warriors at the same time. He sounded the familiar Brisbane wail that prize-fighting was a beastly business. But when he added that it was a heinous sin for such a spectacle to be staged before the eyes of lovely womanhood, I laid down the paper in disgust, and rarely read Mr. Brisbane thereafter.

It seemed to me he was tying his column on a pretty thin premise. Nobody made his companion go to the fight, and since she had wagered several hundred dollars and cheered as loudly as anyone in the amphitheatre, I thought he was deliberately cheating his readers by making her a martyr. But he was a very powerful man and when he died, left an estate of millions, so maybe it was all right. Many a Wall Street broker has talked clients into buying some pretty poor stuff, too.

IV. FEMALE OF THE SPECIES

The weaker sex? Nuts! The dames
can dish it out, and take it, with
more aplomb than any poor male.

IV. FEMALE OF THE SPECIES

I
N THE EARLY DAYS of the twentieth century
one of the most prolific and widely read novelists was a
literary Frank Sinatra named Robert W. Chambers. Mr.

Chambers based the theme of many of his books on the premise that "the best man who ever lived is unworthy of the worst woman." Of course, he was aiming at royalties and not the truth, since he frequently climaxed his tales by having the romantic chambermaid marry a scion of millions. Discontented chambermaids bought his hogwash by the thousands of copies. To prove that he didn't believe the stuff himself, Chambers disinherited a son who married a girl not in the Social Register.

Anyone who even intimates that the best man who ever lived is not worthy of the worst woman is living in an impossible past or is a mental case. It is the same as saying that George Washington, Franklin D. Roosevelt and Dwight Eisenhower are not in the same class with Apple Annie or "Leaping Lena" Levinsky.

There are certain physical and biological differences between men and women. Practically anyone over the age of seven can catalogue these differences. They are interesting in themselves. They have been, and will continue to be, for countless ages, the subject of much study and investigation. They were the bootstraps on which Walter Winchell's "middle-aisling" and "infanticipating," and Earl Wilson's "bosoms, brassieres and behinds" pulled themselves to fame and fortune. There are as many different kinds of women as there are men, and you can run the scale from Madame Curie to Betty Grable to Broadway Rose, with a thousand variations of each.

Cafe Society is essentially a woman's world. All the lovely bar-flies at the Stork Club and the other gin mills, do not spring from the original Vanderbilts, Astors or Whitneys. It is difficult to tell which is which until they take down their hair. Night clubs seem to abound with women in need of weeping walls. Whether or not the giggle-juice makes them that way I don't know, but the false glamour of night club life always seems to attract gilded tramps.

One night I went to Kitty Davis' Airliner on Miami Beach. Louise was sitting at the bar when I came in. Louise is a slim-hipped female, who could make most any movie starlet look like something left over from the night before—and her real name isn't Louise. I had known her when she was a showgirl in New York and practically every playboy in town was laying mink, sables, diamonds and automobiles at her feet. But Louise married a character I will name Glomp, and she dropped out of circulation.

"Hello, Butch," I said. "How are you making it?"

"Well, Jackie boy!" she cried. "Sit down and buy me a drink. I've got to do a little crying and your shoulder is as good as the next."

The crying stuff didn't sound reasonable, for Mr. Glomp had more money than was reasonable or moral. Louise was living luxuriously in Florida, while the dancers who had worked with her were wearing out their feet on the pavement which led from one booking office to another. I mentioned this fact rather casually.

"Men never understand," said Louise, knocking off her Scotch as though it were branch water. "Maybe you will, though, when I get through. Remember when I was playing in 'Bare Facts of 1935?' Well, I married a fellow named Barry Hallett. He was an artist—a good artist, but nobody bought his stuff. We were crazy in love. The moon was made for us, everything was touched with silver and all that sort of thing. Of course, we kept the wedding a secret. It wouldn't have helped the box office if the front-row boys with thin hair and fat billfolds knew I was married.

"Anyway, you know how things go. Barry was the sweetest, most thoughtful person in the world, but I had to have things—things he wouldn't be able to buy me if he lived to be a thousand. We argued and fought, and made up three or four times a week.

"Then, Mr. Glomp came along. I looked him up in Dun and Bradstreet and found that he was worth fifty million dollars if he was worth a dime. His hands were soft and damp and he resembled a drowsy, and none too smart, cocker spaniel. But a girl can't expect Clark Gable with fifty million dollars, can she? Say, bartender, what are you putting in that glass . . . iced tea? Double-up on it, will you?"

It struck me that Louise would not keep her slim hips very long if she handled joy-water that way, but after all, it was her worry, so I said nothing.

"I went to Reno and got my divorce," the girl went on. "It was tough to do and I cried plenty about it, but a woman has to look to the future, you know. She can't live on love. The day I returned to New York, Glomp gave me a hundred thousand dollar check, a star sapphire and a Rolls Royce. He insisted that we run up to New Rochelle right away to get married.

"While I was standing in front of the justice of the peace, I kept saying to myself, 'Why couldn't it have been you, Barry? Why couldn't it have been you?' I looked up into the face of the stupid Gargantua and knew what I had let myself in for. Still, the price wasn't bad.

"After the ceremony we went to Glomp's twenty-room penthouse that looked like a super-special Hollywood set. It must have been the contrast that made me think of the little Greenwich Village dump Barry and I had called home. Say, Jack, you don't think I'm a sentimental fool, do you?"

"No," I said. "No, not exactly sentimental."

"Of course," continued Louise, ignoring my sarcasm, "I had tipped off the gossip columnists, because if I didn't make page one this time I never would. So, while I was going through the cold cream and hair brushing business, I sent the seventh assistant butler out for the morning papers. But I didn't get top billing. The lead story was: 'YOUNG MILLIONAIRE COMMITS SUICIDE . . . Barry Hallett, Greenwich Village artist, who two days ago inherited ten million dollars from an uncle in Australia, shot himself to death today. He left a note in his studio, where the tragedy occurred, to the effect that life without his ex-showgirl wife was not worth living.'

"Just at that moment," Louise went on bitterly, "Glomp bounced gaily in, clean shaven, whistling some irritating tune. He looked even more repulsive than when we were being married. 'What a spot you're in now, baby,' he said, 'what a spot! No more work . . . no more rehearsals . . . everything in the world you want. Are you happy, angel child?'

" 'Everything I want!' I said. 'Ain't it a scream? I'm the happiest woman in the world!' "

After Louise finished her drink I said good-bye. When she became troublesome Danny Davis could handle her. There's such a thing as sticking out your chin, and asking for it!

When I came back from the European Theatre of Operations in November, 1944, I went to La Martinique with lovely Luba Malina, the theatrical nightingale. We both knew a noted comedian who was working there, and we wanted to chat with him.

Along about four in the morning, when business had slowed to a minimum, the comedian, Luba and I settled down to a bit of reminiscing. A member of Cafe Society approached our table. She was tall and blonde, and her evening gown encompassed, but hardly concealed, her charms. I was told later that her ancestors came over in the first section of the Mayflower. Had there been an earlier section, no doubt, they would have boarded that. Her blood was not only blue, but purple.

The lady's approach was in the Duse manner. She had a flair and poise. Her pace was wavering, but dignified. She paused at the table and gave out with a sort of Delsarte motion of the right wrist. In a throaty voice that would be

equally at home in a Park Avenue penthouse or the in-
famous 32 Rue Blondel in Paris, she said to the comedian:
"Look, you stinkin' louse, are you goin' to bed with me,
or aren't you?"

I have been acquainted with members of Murder, Inc.,
owners of what are facetiously known as disorderly houses,
and boss stevedores who were weak enough to get drunk
on a single bottle of bourbon; but I never heard anyone
use the language of this ornament of Cafe Society as she
enlarged on her theme.

Not *all* the feminine indulgers in after-dark life are
out-and-out bums. One of the most colorful night club
personalities the cabaret business ever produced was a
flamboyant female whose natural vivacity and energy
made her early death even more tragic.

Texas Guinan, of course. Her "Hello, sucker!" was
heard around the world. But such was her manner, that
this taunting greeting was always answered with at least
a broad grin.

Many now-famous movie stars started at Guinan's
speakeasy . . . Joan Crawford, who was always getting
into some kind of trouble, Ruby Keeler, Barbara Stan-
wyck and other eyefuls, danced, at one time or another,
in her chorus line. Some wound up marrying truck
drivers or millionaires, others committed suicide, but these
three smart girls went on to movie fame and greater for-
tunes than garrulous Guinan ever dreamed of. Oddly

enough, for girls who made their start in a chorus, they saved their money.

Perhaps Eva Tanguay was a lesson to them; maybe they never even heard of her. I don't know. Young show people are indifferent to the history of their trade. But I remember Eva, though from a day when I could only adore, not approach.

She was a pretty, scintillating comedienne, who rode to fame on the lyric of a song called, "I Don't Care." Like other young women, who never before had anything and suddenly have everything, success went to her head. She developed temperament, which means nothing more than selfishness, bad manners, and a trend toward exhibitionism. She walked out on performances and contracts. Eva threw away her money like the proverbial drunken sailor. She was convinced that she could always make more.

Now deep in her 60s, Eva Tanguay has been blind and crippled for years. She has existed only through the generosity of such old timers as Sophie Tucker, "the Last of the Red Hot Mammas." But sick, blind, penniless and old, Eva Tanguay is as imperious and demanding as ever.

So you see, though Robert W. Chambers was certainly able to throw an adverb around, he didn't know such a hell of a lot about women. Either that, or they were different in 1910 than they are now, which I doubt. Tap the so-called gentle sex of any given era, and you'll find that fundamentally they don't vary.

But they are all interesting. And I was out to meet interesting people.

V. IT COULD BE SPORT

Sports are oftimes a synthetic drama. But sometimes Fate turns phoniness into very real tragedy.

V. IT COULD BE SPORT

THERE IS an ancient story with a bald head and long white whiskers that has been a favorite of mine for many years. It concerns an old Greek fruit peddler, who landed in the United States with two dollars and eleven cents in his pocket. After many years it was bruited about that he was worth half a million. The local newspaper sent a reporter to write the success story.

"Why, shush," said the old Greek. "She is true, this story. I come to the Unired Steps. I doan shine shoes. I doan open ristarant for rosbif and stromberry pie. I sell fruit. All day I sell fruit. First I get pusher-cart, then little store. All day I wark from fiver clock in morning to twelver clock at night, just selling fruit. Thirty years I do this . . . and then my grandmother dies, and lives me five hunnerd thousand dollars!"

Of course, some characters have gained affluence that way, but most people only achieve it by sweat.

One fellow who did it the hard way was a stone mason of Frioul, Italy, named Ottavio Bottechia. He was thin and ungainly, not unlike a crane in profile; with gimlet eyes and a nose like a pickaxe. More than anything else in the world he wanted money. Money became an obsession with him, and there was little to be made with mallet and chisel. Then, Ottavio had an inspiration. He would ride in the Tour de France, which was the cycling Iliad of Europe before the war.

Each year, in the baking heat of July, the athletes pedaled their push-bikes around the borders of France in a race that took a month to complete. It was called the "convict's job" . . . but it was more than that. Even those who toiled in the bush of the penal colony in French Guiana were not called upon for more numbing toil.

The participants pedaled the lonely roads of Brittany, where white coiffed women stared at them with wide eyes. Here wayside shrines are nestled in the cool shade, and the people pray in a tongue that is strange to Parisian Frenchmen. But even these people know of the Tour de France, and call riders by their names, urging them on with shouts of, "Hardie, Coco!"

Then, the cyclists are out of Brittany, and struggling over the shoulders of the Basque country. White coifs and the traditional gloom of the peasant disappear. Here are woodchoppers with bandannas, pirate-style, around their foreheads. But the seekers after fortune hardly notice. They are bound to their wheels.

Up those hills high-powered automobiles struggle in second gear. Human legs must strain, and blood gorge the eyes, as the men in the Tour de France push their cycles up . . . up . . . up . . .

Suddenly that is past, too, and the pack is in the dusty Midi. Crowds block the roads, cheering. Everyone is immensely enthusiastic and gay. Then comes the rise and slide of the Crau, the switchbacks of Savoy and the lower Alps, Alsace, the black roads of the North country . . . and so into Paris.

This is the trail . . . and the cyclist covers it alone. He patches his tires, and bandages his wounds himself. Under no circumstances is he permitted aid, under penalty of disqualification. Officials patrol the road in automobiles. A man is continually under surveillance . . . but alone . . . utterly alone.

He burns out his heart and soul and body in the effort, but how could he earn 60 thousand francs otherwise . . . in a day when 60 thousand francs was a great fortune?

Bottechia thought of that. Money dazzled him. No matter what happened, he must have it. His friends told him he was mad. There was not one chance in a million that he could win.

There was iron in Ottavio's soul. He knew what obstacles stood between him and the 60 thousand francs, but he was not discouraged. He drew his thin savings from the bank. That whole, golden fall he spent riding over the route of the race, and studying it. He found where he must burn himself out, and where he might be able to save his strength.

When race time came the professionals paid no attention to him. Bottechia was an amateur . . . an interloper. They had nothing to fear from him. But to the astonishment of everyone, Ottavio finished second. It nearly killed him. Lying in bed, the thought of next year hastened recovery. Second prize money paid for his training and gave him a nest egg to work on.

Though he despised the business, Bottechia saw in it his only escape from poverty. He hated the professionals and they hated him. They wallowed thigh deep in applause. They sucked it up as though they were sponges. Ottavio cared nothing for public appreciation. All he wanted was money.

He started in his second race . . . this sallow skeleton in

his yellow jersey . . . and this time the veterans knew he was a man to watch.

The pace was murderous. Pellisier was the first of the champions to fall by the roadside. He was great in his day, but age had taken its toll. Old Alavoine crumbled before the Pyrenees were reached, and many had wagered their last francs on him.

It was on those savage slopes that the mason made his bid for victory. His stringy legs pumped ceaselessly. His mouth was dry, his lips cracked. There was a knife between his shoulder blades that made each sucking breath a torture. He fell, and rose again, and the skin split into the flesh. Salt sweat burned his wounds. He was saddle sore and every muscle ached, but he rode harder.

Even the rugged Belgians fell hopelessly behind. Only Brunero, grimacing with weariness, held on through the little villages of the Alps. Before Strasbourg was reached, even his endurance gave out. No one could match the cold fanaticism of the mason from Frioul.

At last Bottechia rode into Paris alone. His face was a dust-covered mask of agony, runneled with sweat. His ribs showed through the skin, and his stomach was that of a bad sailor in a heavy storm.

As he pedaled through the hot, packed streets, he was overwhelmed with a delirium of applause. The boulevardiers had hoped a Frenchman would win, but since an Italian had shown the way, they were quite willing to salute him.

Pretty girls smiled and tossed flowers to Ottavio . . .

the heroic scarecrow, who had been a laughingstock in his own home town. But he didn't care about the applause, or the pretty girls, or the glory.

Ottavio had endured torments for 60 thousand francs . . . and when you stop to think of it, this motive, which sounds ignoble, is the same one that drives us through our days. Inside, we're all a little like the mason of Frioul, though we may not be as courageous or calculating.

That makes me think of a cafe in Berlin . . . when there was a Berlin. The air was heavy from long-stemmed pipes and atrocious cigars. Nearly everyone was drinking beer and eating.

Fat men, with sweaty red faces . . . Lean, hard men, very stiff in the back, who clicked their heels and bowed from the waist . . . Here and there a cheek with the old-fashioned saber slash . . . Waiters moved quietly about, balancing trays . . . Traffic roared past the windows . . . A band played *Zwei Herzen im dreiviertal Takt* . . . The feet of dancers shuffled a litany of pleasure . . . Lovers touched lips and squeezed hands.

At eleven o'clock the manager went from table to table, speaking in undertones to his regular patrons. One by one they drifted toward the back room. This was to be a scene not fit for everyone . . . a fight to the finish between two women.

If you have illusions and your stomach is squeamish, you won't want to see women fight. There is something too elemental about their anger and determination. But

63

these men wanted to see feminine flesh beaten with fists, so their nerve ends would twitch with thrills.

The back room was fitted with a ring in the approved manner. Benches occupied every other available inch of space. These benches were filled with men. Some looked embarrassed, almost ashamed. The eyes of others shone wetly and they licked their lips.

The fighters entered. One had taffy colored hair and pink cheeks. She came from Hesse. Her breasts were big and round, the wonderful breasts of a potential mother.

The other's hair was black as pitch, and her tanned skin almost sallow. The men, undressing the girls with their eyes, saw that her breasts were small and pointed and hard, and her tights fitted closely in the V of her crotch. The girls' legs were not bunched with muscle, but smooth and shapely, as they should be. They were about twenty years old.

They were greeted with handclapping and dirty remarks. The woman from Hesse paid no attention. But the black haired girl, who was the daughter of a mill worker in Berlin North, said in a thin voice: "You bastards . . . oh, you bastards!"

The referee, an indecent, wrinkled man in a dinner jacket, explained that the fight would be under Marquis of Queensberry rules, except that there would be no hitting on the breasts. He snickered as he said it.

Someone struck a bell. They went toward each other, left hands extended, right high, guarding the jaw. Their small feet shifted impatiently, kicking up the resin. They were quick and seemed to have some knowledge of boxing. Though neither suffered much damage in the first few rounds, it was apparent that the Berliner was stronger. The blond girl was made for loving; not such work as this.

In the fourth round it became ugly. Taffy-hair split her opponent's lips with a hard smash. A blot of blood filmed her white teeth, and dripped down onto her jersey. The Berliner was infuriated. She attacked like a mad cat, swinging furiously with both hands.

The blond's hair escaped its fastenings and tumbled about her shoulders. Those men who were not perverts thought how nice it would be to run their fingers through its golden glory. But none of them thought how nice it would be to kiss her. Her mouth was swollen and sticky with blood.

Suddenly the girl fell forward on her hands and knees. She sobbed, and strained for breath. The referee began to count. The Hessian drew her slim legs under her, and rose. Her enemy took one step toward her, then struck. Yellow-head fell forward, her arms hardly breaking the fall. She hit the canvas with a thud.

That was a sight not soon to be forgotten. The blond on the floor, head on her arms, blood forming a little pool under her face . . . the Berliner looking down with an almost savage smile.

Seconds picked up the inert body and carried it to the corner. The blond girl opened her eyes, and began to cry. The men with the monocles and bored lips threw silver and paper money into the ring. Then they shuffled out.

In the big room the band started playing *Zwei Herzen im dreiviertal Takt* again. Couples were dancing gracefully, and women were being seduced or, in their turn, seducing.

But the little girl in her woolen shirt and shorts brushed the blood from her face, and wept uncomforted.

That, too, had been done for money.

Money is important, of course, and there would be no professional sport without money, but there are stories about the play-for-pay men that have nothing to do with hard cash.

It may be that you know nothing of jai alai . . . the Basque sport that is played in only one American city, Miami. It is the fastest of all games, and I have seen them all. There is nothing quite like it, a sort of inter-marriage of handball and court tennis. The players catch and throw the hard ball with an odd shaped wicker basket called a cesta, strapped to the right hand. The ball travels at 100 miles an hour. Since the court is 178 feet long, tremendous speed and stamina is required to cover it.

There are no American players. They are all Spaniards, Mexicans, Cubans, with a sprinkling of Brazilians. It seems to me, of all the stories I have heard about jai alai players, that of Pedro Garate is the most dramatic.

In 1936 Pedro was playing at the Biscayne Fronton. James J. Braddock was asked to present a cup to the winner of a special game. Pedro was the victor, and obliging Jim posed for photographs with him.

Next year the boxing champion returned to Miami, and

went to the fronton for an evening of excitement. Pedro approached, and kissed his hand. Now, cavaliers may go about brushing the fingers of lovely ladies with their lips, but not the scarred knuckles of prize-fighters.

Braddock said, "What the hell is this all about?"

"You saved my life," answered Pedro.

"What is this . . . a gag?"

"By no means a gag. After you presented me with the trophy last March, I went to Madrid to visit my family. The city was being bombed. All one heard were sirens, explosions and the typewriter sound of machine guns.

"Madrid was in panic. The secret police were arresting thousands for espionage . . . and firing squads of the military tribunals were busy day after day. One afternoon the police came to my father's house, and arrested me. My family begged and pleaded. We were known for our loyalty to the government, but that was not enough.

"The police hustled me off. I was herded into a barracks with other miserable wretches . . . men and women . . . rich and poor . . . students and peasants. A little later I was taken before a court martial. The officers were tired; some were wounded. They had become blase over the tragic farce of sending people to their deaths.

"They listened in a bored way to my denials. The senior officer announced that I had been found guilty, and would be shot the next morning. Guards hustled me back to prison.

"I am not a coward, Senor Braddock, but I died a thousand deaths that night. At five o'clock in the morning

I heard the clump, clump, of the execution squad. I pictured myself standing before a bullet-pitted wall, trying to smoke a last cigaret.

"Out of the dawn came the dry crash of a volley . . . a minute later a single pistol shot blew out the brains of a victim. I called the sergeant of the guard. I spoke of the standing of my family . . . its loyalty . . . my love of Spain. Let the tribunal hear me once more. The sergeant was soft-hearted and the officers agreed to listen to me.

"When I was brought into the big bare room the colonel looked coldly at me through his glasses.

" 'If you have anything to say, say it quickly,' he commanded in a voice like dry sawdust.

"Then it came to me like a message from heaven. In my pocket was a newspaper clipping of Jim Braddock presenting Pedro with a silver cup. I laid it on the desk.

" 'Look, senor colonel,' I told him, 'This is James J. Braddock, the boxing champion. This is me. I am a player of the jai alai. You must believe I am telling the truth.'

"The colonel and the others studied the pictures. He said: 'It is incontrovertible. Release him, guards' . . . and added: 'If Pedro is a friend of Jim Braddock I would release him if he were Franco's brother. I won a thousand pesos from General Gomez on that boxer!' So," concluded Pedro, "that is why I kiss your hand, Senor Braddock."

There is tragedy in sport, too, as there is in every enterprise known to man. Tragedy is a great part of race track lore. Around the tracks one finds gallantry and crookedness; amazing reversals of form. No one knew the saga of the thoroughbreds better than Sam Hildreth, one of the great trainers of all time, a man of mind and heart. Yes, and a storyteller, too, with the gift of words when he wanted to use them.

The feuds between race tracks in the 1940s is no more bitter than the mild jealousy of women whose hats are too startlingly similar. But it wasn't so in the old days, when the oat burners ran and the gamblers bet, at Hawthorne and Garfield in Chicago.

Old Sam Hildreth told me about that battle one star-spangled August night on the veranda of the United States Hotel in Saratoga.

Ed Corrigan operated Hawthorne, in what was later to be crime-smeared Cicero. George V. Hankins opened Garfield Park in opposition. This was back in 1892. Mike McDonald, Chicago's Democratic boss gave lusty backing to Hankins, and Mayor Washburn supported Corrigan.

Among the owners who stabled horses at Garfield was a little man, wrinkled and tanned and thin as a straw wisp. Twenty years before he had been sheriff of Lee County, Texas, and it was said that he could draw a gun faster than any man on earth.

Peace officers needed speed on the draw, or their lives ended quickly and messily. It seemed no happy omen for Jim Brown when Wesley Hardin and Bill Langley, two of the worst killers Texas ever knew, appeared in Lee County. The little man went after them, and when the blaze of gunfire ended, Hardin was dead and Langley a prisoner.

Eventually Brown turned in his badge, and took to racing horses. In September, 1892, he brought his thoroughbreds to Garfield. Jim was very mild, but had a hairspring temper. All he wanted was to be left alone to mind his own business. It was his credo not to interfere with other people's affairs.

The political squabble between the tracks was no concern of the ex-sheriff's. But trouble rose to a crescendo when Mayor Washburn sent 200 policemen to raid Garfield and arrest everyone.

From Jim Brown's point of view, this was not playing the game. When the bluecoats came swarming in, the little man stood his ground. He had never run from anyone in his life. He didn't intend to now.

A patrolman named John Powell, red-faced and mustached in the Chicago tradition, approached threateningly. In his warm, soft voice, Brown warned Powell to stay away. But the policeman, because he had been warned this man was dangerous, pulled his gun and fired at the former sheriff's feet.

Something snapped in Jim. Out came his own gun, and Powell lay dead on the ground, a bullet through his mouth.

The man who had brought the law to Lee County knew he was going to die at the hands of the law. He began running toward the 40th Street gate, though with no thought in mind that he would ever make it. Policeman Henry MacDowell, Powell's partner, circled a barn, and caught up with the wiry old man. He grabbed Brown by the throat, his fingers sinking deep.

Sheriff Jim had no great physical strength. He couldn't get away from that grip. He felt his brain snapping under pressure. But it was not difficult to shove the muzzle of his .44 against MacDowell's belly, and squeeze the trigger.

In an instant Brown was waveringly on his feet. There was no way out. Everywhere he looked, policemen were converging on him. The little blue-grey eyes in the tanned face swept over them with almost an appraising look.

There was only a moment left in which to live. In that moment Jim must have thought of his horses . . . of Bobby Beach, who had won 15 out of 18 races . . . Annie M, Red Banner, G. W. Johnson . . . all thoroughbreds, who had carried his colors. He would never see them again. He, who had kept the law so well, would die at the hands of the law, branded as a murderer.

Half a dozen policemen fired at the same time. Jim felt hot lead sear his body. His knees buckled, though his eyes were fixed unflinchingly on his foes. Then he fell. His shirt front was sticky with blood. There was the welt of a bullet across his forehead.

Jim Grant, an old friend, ran to him. Brown half raised the old .44.

"For God's sake, you're not going to shoot me, are you?" Grant cried, falling on his knees beside the old warrior.

The veteran peace officer was breathing heavily.

"No . . . no, shore not," he gasped. "But here's one more bullet for that . . . son of a bitch . . ."

He tried to point the gun at a policeman who had fired at him from behind the barn, but there wasn't strength in his finger to squeeze the trigger.

So, the ex-peace officer of Lee County, Texas, died at the hands of the peace officers of Cook County, Illinois.

VI. GAME OF CHANCE

The saga of "Wingy" Grober and some of his cohorts, the percentage boys.

VI. GAME OF CHANCE

FROM THE WAY the words are used inter-
changeably, it might appear at first glance that "personality" and "character" mean exactly the same thing. This is

74

far from being the case. For instance, Lt. Gen. Ira C. Eaker, on whose staff I served with the 8th Air Force, and Col. John Hay Whitney, my section chief, were personalities, but certainly not characters.

New York is full . . . and most other cities have their quotas . . . of out-and-out characters. "Swifty" Morgan, who wanders about the country selling neckties and diamonds with equal aplomb; "Frisco Legs," who is known as "the Nation's Guest" because, while he spends winters in Miami and summers in Atlantic City — comfortably, if not opulently — he has no visible means of support; "El Goofy" Gomez, the once great left-handed pitcher of the New York Yankees, whose wisecracks and thin batting average became baseball history; "Broadway Rose," the faded flower of the Main Stem and other such people. These are characters, under the Damon Runyon definition. If they have added nothing to the knowledge or morality of the world, they have added something to its gaiety.

Gambling, as a business, has developed few colorful characters. But an exception to this is a fellow named "Wingy" Grober, a night club operator on Miami Beach. Wingy has been risking his money at horses, roulette, dice, or any other game of chance, since he outgrew his desk in the third grade. Wingy is full of stories. He has a million of them, and some are unquestionably true. Even before Mr. Grober became a citizen of Miami, he was a steady visitor at Hialeah during the winter season. This was before the mutuel machines were installed.

One morning during a season not too many years ago, Wingy drifted into the lobby of the Fleetwood hotel where he was staying. The winter day was sunny and warm but the little man felt no uplift from Nature's gentle gifts. The bookmakers at Hialeah had stripped him clean and picked his financial bones. Mr. Grober had two nickels in his pants pockets, and owed a month's rent at the hotel.

Hunger nibbled at his vitals, but breakfast was a luxury beyond his means. At the cigar stand he spent one of his nickels for a copy of the Miami *Herald*, not because world news interested him, but, being a gambler, he could not bear to start the day without knowing what horses were running.

This reduced his assets to a shiny five cent piece, which was as useful to him as a single lipstick to a Ubangi woman. There was a slot machine next to the cigar counter. Wingy dropped in his nickel. He hit the jackpot, and found himself enriched to the amount of six dollars and twenty cents.

"This," muttered Mr. Grober to himself as he entered a cafeteria to reinforce his tissues "is my day. I feel it in my bones."

He had a pass to Hialeah, and free transportation in a friend's car. A more prudent man might have stashed away a dollar or two against unforeseen contingencies, but not Wingy. He bet five dollars on a 20-to-1 shot in the first race, which won going away. On the wings of an incredible burst of luck, the little man won seven straight races. When he returned to the Fleetwood that night, his pockets bulged with nine thousand dollars in folding money.

Grober paid the long overdue hotel bill, staked acquaintances who were as broke as he had been that morning, and then edged himself into a crap game. When dawn peeped through the venetian blinds, he had sixteen thousand dollars.

After running a nickel into this amount, it might seem that the little man would be satisfied. But he could no more go without gambling than he could without food. By the time the meeting at Hialeah was over, Wingy Grober had nearly forty grand in the bank.

There were other race meetings . . . other crap games. The little man tracked North, and Lady Luck was still his constant companion. No one knew better than he that she is a fickle jade, likely to turn without warning on those she has showered with favors. By the time Saratoga opened, Mr. Grober decided to hedge. Having run a nickel into sixty-five thousand dollars, he went over to the opposite side of the fence. In conjunction with another gambler, he opened a "book" in New York's famous Spa.

The business was moderately, but not sensationally, successful. Then, on the last day of the meeting, the favorite in every race came home in front. By the time he paid off, and bought a railroad ticket to New York, Wingy had something less than two dollars!

Not even that shook his confidence. But money to a gambler is the equivalent of tools to a carpenter or a plumber — he can't function without it.

That fall Wingy found himself in Havre de Grace. The little town was jammed. He had somehow amassed six

77

hundred dollars as working capital and hoped to build it into a sizeable sum. One night Grober ran into a tout he knew, an ex-jockey called "Homeless," who was known as an incurable thief. The November evening had turned cold, and Homeless shivered under his threadbare jacket.

"Let me sleep in your room tonight, Wingy," he begged. "I'll freeze to death if I don't. I ain't got no dough, and even if I had, I wouldn't be able to get a place." He looked forlorn and tired, and Grober owns a soft heart, in spite of his bluster. He didn't want any part of Homeless, for he knew his bankroll was in danger, but he couldn't turn the fellow down.

They prepared for bed, while the wind's chilled fingers tapped on the glass. Wingy gave serious thought to places he could hide his money, for Homeless would begin his search sometime during the night. Though Grober admits that the only thing which prevented him from going into the fourth grade was the third grade, he is a practical psychologist. Suddenly, the perfect solution came to him.

Homeless would undoubtedly wait until nearly dawn before attempting to steal the roll. When the tout drifted off to sleep, Wingy slid out of bed and hid his money. Then he climbed back and was soon asleep.

It was morning when he awoke. Homeless, a cigaret pasted to his lower lip, and a gloomy expression on his weazened face, was wandering aimlessly about the room in his underwear. Wingy grinned at him.

"Bad luck, huh?" he asked. "You couldn't find my roll, could you?"

Homeless shrugged his shoulders. "No," he admitted. "Where the hell did you hide it?"

Wingy sat up in bed. "In the one place you'd never look, bum . . . in your pants pocket! Now, beat it, before I bust you over the noggin with this shoe!"

Miami, and the adjacent Beach, became a haven for strange characters during prohibition days. A good many engaged in rum-running, because Nassau and Bimini were close at hand. The gang lords came for the racing, the night clubs and the sun, and stayed for the smuggling. They were not wanted, and when they finally disappeared from the scene, it was not due to an act of God, but to the energy of John Edgar Hoover of the Federal Bureau of Investigation. Hoover's smart young men shot a lot of these characters and put others behind bars for years and years. This improved conditions no end.

However, there were many interesting people, utterly unknown to either the law or the headlines. They did the best they could to earn a dollar; sometimes honestly, sometimes in opposition to the Eighteenth Amendment.

One of these chaps was a quiet and unobtrusive baldheaded man, who was naturally called Curly. He later entered the restaurant business. Curly, a jovial personality, did most of the cooking himself, because he was better at the stove than any chef he could hire.

The reason for the gentleman's selection of a career as a Cordon Bleu is worth recording.

Back in 1923 Curly owned a speakeasy on Ocean Drive

and Second Street at Miami Beach. At the start, he had no idea of opening a joint. He had left school when he was sixteen and batted about the country, trying his hand at anything that came along.

In 1919 he found himself in Miami. Everybody's brother was a bootlegger, so Curly decided to join up, too.

The Coast Guard was doing its sweaty best to ruin the traffic, but they would have needed the entire navy to make headway against the fleets that ran stock from Bimini, Nassau and Jamaica.

The Guardsmen succeeded in one thing. They upset Curly's nerves. By the time he opened his speakeasy, he had become as bald as an egg. He always declared a Coast Guard shell had given him a hundred percent part down the middle of the skull. This cured him of the sea, and having no inconsiderable sum of money, Curly opened his retail establishment.

As a camouflage, he hung a "Steaks and Chops" sign out front. There wasn't a crust of bread in the place, but somehow the authorities were allergic to bootleggers displaying a placard inscribed "Fine Wines and Liquors."

One evening three gentlemen stalked in. They had an official air, being flatfooted and hawkeyed. Curly didn't like their deportment. He suffered from unvoiced suspicions. These guys were G-men, he was sure.

They didn't ask for liquor. The biggest one said: "A planked steak for three, well done." It seemed to Curly that there was an ominous and threatening note in the man's voice.

"Yes, sir," said the proprietor. He went into the kitchen, straight through the back door into the home of a neighbor.

"Look, Joe," he said, "I'm on a spot. Three rev'nooers are in my joint, askin' for a steak. You got one?"

The neighbor understood the exigencies of running a speakeasy. He had been in the business himself.

"There's one in the ice box," he said, "but the old lady will raise hell when she comes back and finds it gone. Well, let her. I never let a pal down yet."

Curly seized the beef, raced back to his kitchen, lit the fire, and tossed his prize on the pan. When it was done, he served it. The three official looking men went to work, and being good trenchermen, left nothing.

"Boy," said the spokesman, "you're quite a cook. That's as good a steak as ever gave my bridgework a tussle. We'll have to tell the folks back in Cleveland about this place."

Curly smiled nervously.

"Now, look, gentlemen," he said, "it's probably none of my business, but what business are you in?"

"We're shoe manufacturers!" they chorused. And they really were.

But Curly never became discouraged. He lost his shirt on the horses. He lost his hair running rum. He was chased out of the speakeasy business because he mistook shoe manufacturers for government agents.

"It's all right," he said, "if I hadn't fumbled that one I might never have found out I could cook. That would have been real tragedy."

It would have been a tragedy for many gourmets and

epicures. Curly had a way with a steak that approached genius. He was, as far as culinary skill is concerned, an artist.

There is no end to fellows who have had experiences with that cross-eyed old beldame Lady Luck and found her favors are not to be taken lightly.

There was a lad named Frenchy, who, when I met him, was working at the service bar in Sam Barken's Five O'Clock Club, on Miami Beach.

Back in 1918, Frenchy was engaged as a waiter at the Club Dore in San Francisco. Money was as loose as a call-girl's morals, and Frenchy was doing all right for himself, even though the fellows in the Argonne were not exactly having a tea party.

One night he had a party of six well-dressed, glossy men. At five in the morning they decided to call it a day. The most sober one called for the check. He paid it, then reached into his pocket and pulled out a five thousand dollar Liberty Bond. "Thish is for you waiter," he mumbled.

Frenchy didn't want to split that colossal tip with the head waiter and he did what nine men out of ten would do. He said, "Thank you, sir," and stashed away the bond. The only trouble was that the generous guest was George Coster, who headed a ring smuggling Chinamen into the United States. A couple of hours later George was found in a gutter, with a knife between his shoulder blades.

This Coster was a wrong gee, but crime is crime. The police rounded up everybody in the Club Dore, and found the five thousand dollar bond—made out in Coster's name—on Frenchy. That was all they needed. They tossed him into the clink, charged with murder.

The waiter was in a panic. He told his story, and they laughed at him. Later they didn't laugh. They went to work on him with blackjacks and a rubber hose. But he didn't have anything more to tell.

A couple of weeks later the lieutenant came in, and said: "We're gonna let you out, Frenchy."

"Let me out?" he said. "I thought you had a murder rap pinned on me. Why, after you guys finished goin' over me I looked like a patchwork quilt. I've lost five years off the good end of my life."

"It was all in fun," said the lieutenant. "You mustn't mind little things like that."

The lieutenant patted Frenchy on the back. He had a hand like a ham, and the waiter had felt the knuckles on his jaw when he was getting what the newspapers call a "severe questioning."

Well, it seems that the head waiter had seen Coster pass Frenchy the bond. He had his back turned, but he was looking into a mirror and didn't miss a thing. He was sore because he hadn't been given his share, but finally told the story. If he hadn't, Frenchy might have burned in the hot seat.

The waiter was released. He figured five grand wasn't bad pay for what he had gone through . . . but then what happened? The head waiter was waiting, asking for his fifty-fifty cut. He made his subordinate sell the bond, and count him in for half.

So, when I knew Frenchy, the lad was working at the Five O'Clock Club, in the service bar, where a customer doesn't give tips. He figured five thousand dollar tips weren't healthy.

Most characters are not important in the doings of the world. A good many are fascinating; some are boring, even though unique. The bores are those who have developed a mania for publicity. A few, like "Titanic" Thompson, have no desire to see their names in print.

Thompson was a professional gambler, and some of the best known characters on Broadway were men of his ignoble profession. They think in terms of odds and percentages, even in their love affairs.

Titanic became immensely interested in golf. He spent his nights gambling and his days on the links, either playing, taking lessons, or practicing.

Well, Titanic Thompson joined the Grassy Sprain Golf Club in Bronxville, New York, and worked arduously at improving his score. Like most gamblers, he had the gift of intense concentration. His game improved day by day and soon he was playing regularly in the middle 70s.

The club's professional was a veteran named George McLean. Though George had never won a major championship, he knew every blade of grass on his home course, and was practically unbeatable there. Because he believed it would help his game to compete with an expert, Thompson went around with McLean three or four times a week, and continually improved.

It wasn't long until the professional was giving his ambitious opponent a handicap of only two strokes. They played regularly for one hundred dollars a round, but McLean invariably won by a narrow margin.

After one of these duellos, Titanic remarked that he could not get steamed to the proper pitch playing for chicken feed. Naturally, George asked what Mr. Thompson would consider a reasonable sum.

"About ten grand," the gambler muttered casually.

Of course, the golf professional had no such cash reserve. The club members, however, had implicit faith in George, so a pool was organized. McLean took five hundred dollars of it himself, and was promised a cut on everybody's winnings, if he were the victor.

The match was a tight, well-played one. Coming to the last tee, they were even. McLean hit a magnificent second shot to within four feet of the pin. His heart was high and happy, for while Thompson also landed on the green, his ball was at least forty feet from the cup.

There was no change in the gambler's expression. It was as composed as usual. Almost casually he gauged the line, and hit his ball squarely into the can!

That broke McLean's heart and nerve. Suddenly the four footer that had looked so easy a moment before, assumed the proportions of the Grand Canyon. With ten thousand dollars hanging on that putt, the professional probably could not have sunk it from six inches.

So, Titanic won the ten grand, but the money didn't matter. More than once he had bet five times that amount on a roll of the dice. His satisfaction lay in beating McLean, and for a moment he even allowed a faintly sardonic smile to shadow his thin lips.

That is the gambling spirit. I have seen "Nick the Greek" and the late Arnold Rothstein, wager sums that would take an average man twenty years to earn. They won or lost without betraying the slightest joy or anger. Their hearts were ice and their blood carbolic acid.

Rothstein, you'll remember, was mysteriously shot to death in front of a crowd that never would talk. So far as the police are concerned, that murder is still unsolved. At least, no one has ever been convicted of it. "Big George" McManus was arrested on suspicion of homicide, but after a while he was let out on bail.

The only person who lingered behind bars was an old Irish scrubwoman, who was held as a material witness. She had no more to do with that killing than Rita Hayworth had with the conquest of Okinawa, but she was tossed into the brig and kept there, while the accused man had his fun on Broadway. But that was just one of the strange quirks of our laws.

VII. THE DESPERADOES

The gimme guys who plundered their way to wealth. Get in their way, and you kissed this world goodbye.

VII. THE DESPERADOES

THE GANGSTER is not entirely indigenous to the United States. Every country in the world has its quota of thieves, killers and blackmailers. There was only one fundamental difference between the millionaire gangsters of other years: Al Capone, Dutch Schultz, Owney Madden or Lepke Buchalter, and the Bulgarian bandit or Montmartre apache. It was one of organizing ability. Crime was big business to the Americans.

For a time some of these leaders achieved the anonymity they craved. Headlines went to thick-headed, trigger-crazy men like John Dillinger, "Baby Face" Nelson and Alvin Karpis. They were as old-fashioned in their methods as Jesse James. Each was listed successively as Public Enemy Number One, the equivalent of a death sentence. They were hunted out by John Edgar Hoover and his agents of the Federal Bureau of Investigation. One by one they were shot to death, or sent to prison for life.

The organizers were harder to get. They assembled batteries of morally dubious, but mentally alert, barristers, tax agents and other experts to keep them out of trouble. This, in the long run, was quite impossible, and they finished just as unhappily as the foot-loose killers. Schultz was murdered, Buchalter electrocuted, and Capone, after years in Alcatraz, became a mental and physical wreck.

I knew these men, and scores like them. They had no redeeming qualities, not even a sense of humor. They were vermin on the body politic, and wrote a dirty history of their own with machine guns and bribes. But some are discussed in this informal recording, because they were a definite, if unpleasant part, of the American pattern. They took up much of the time of newspapermen. Their activities were covered from their beginnings until they ended in the gutter or the electric chair.

Few gangsters were able to keep any considerable percentage of their ill-gotten gains. When Boo Boo Hoff, who operated on a large scale in the Philadelphia-Atlantic City area with Mickey Duffy, passed into the great beyond, he bequeathed his widow an estate of $300. Most of his fellows were similarly improvident.

Boo Boo attempted to mask his larcenous enterprises by acting as a manager of prize fighters. In this connection he was a frequent visitor to the sports department of the Philadelphia newspapers. Hoff fascinated our hunch-backed office boy, Hughey McLoon. Hughey, with his pixie face and a smile like the sunrise, had lived in slum poverty all his short life. But he was ambitious.

He quit the paper, and went to work for the Duffy-Hoff combine. I saw McLoon occasionally around Philadelphia, Atlantic City and New York. He always attended the fights and wrestling matches, because, being a crooked back, he had an almost morbid admiration for athletes. Hughey wore tailored clothes and a diamond ring, and was invariably accompanied by a willowy blond who towered above his twisted frame. He began to drink, and in liquor, lost his sunrise smile; he became turbulent and noisy.

"You're a sucker to trail with that mob," I said. "What's it going to get you?"

He grinned. "You sound like Father Madigan. Neither of you know what you're talkin' about. I got eighteen dollars a week at the *Ledger*, and had to give most of it to my old woman. Now, money's the cheapest thing in the world. I got pocketsful of it. Look at that broad of mine. Ain't she a dish? You ask me what this game's gonna get me! Just what I got . . . and it's enough. Besides, did you ever hear of a guy with a hump livin' to be an old man? Today's long enough to figure on. How do you know you're gonna be here tomorrow?"

McLoon's warped philosophy worked out. Several months later his bullet riddled body was found in the areaway of a West Philadelphia hotel. He had always talked too much. This time he had talked in the wrong place. There were others like him: boys who became fascinated by the wealth and swank of the hoodlums and tried to be like them. On the other hand, some people don't like that sort of thing.

When Eddie Schaffer broke into show business in 1940 he was hired by the toughest joint in Brooklyn, the Bali Club.

This hobby lobby of Murder, Inc., was run by Lepke Buchalter. Schaffer didn't know this. He was glad to get a chance, and grabbed the forty-a-week Lepke so generously offered.

"Loop Benny," a Chicago gunman linked with Murder, Inc., had watched Schaffer clowning during his half-hour lunch period, while Eddie was running skins for a fur house. Benny thought the boy was terrific, and brought him to the Brooklyn joint. Schaffer wasn't there long before he realized the set-up. Broken-nosed characters who slugged guests, beady-eyed gunmen, hulking bruisers —all pointed to the score. Eddie, unfortunately, became a hit. The gang was convulsed by his gags. They thought so much of him, that if customers didn't laugh they were clipped by waiters.

The boys couldn't do enough for the comic. There was a car with a chauffeur at his disposal. They were solicitous about what he ate and drank. They gave him a "hot" diamond ring, and often they asked, "Eddie, what can we do for your family? Maybe a case of whisky for your mudder, Eddie, huh?"

Schaffer asked for a raise, and got it. A ten dollar one. Incidentally, he never did rise higher than $80 a week because the boys didn't want to spoil him.

But Eddie, after the sixth Brooklyn murder caused the club to close for a night or two, decided he had enough.

He asked for a release. The mob was aghast. "Leave us, Eddie, after we made you?" Schaffer said he didn't care. Six months was long enough at one place.

The boys talked to Eddie, "If you leave and go to Toledo, we get you. Same in Chi or Cinncy or L.A."

A bruiser advanced on Eddie while several others held him. "You wouldn't want me to poke you in the eye with this cigar, Eddie, would you?" he asked. So saying, he poked Eddie in the eye. If the butt hadn't been dead, Schaffer would have become a one-eyed comedian.

So he stayed. Then, a few months later, Schaffer got an

idea. He had planned a nose operation to pretty up his horn, and asked the bosses for an okay.

They said sure. Eddie got the operation and planned to stay in the hospital as long as he could. Ten days later the boys came up.

The comic had his nose in bandages. "When you coming back, Eddie?" they asked.

Schaffer said it would be weeks before he could take off the bandages. "Oh, dat's nothin'," they said airily. "You're funnier wit' 'em. Come along." Eddie got up and went to work.

After a year, Schaffer asked for a vacation. Guinea Rocco shook his head. "We gotta do something wit' you, Eddie," he said thoughtfully. Six of them dragged the boy down to the basement. A hand struck sharply, and there were five angry red marks across his cheek.

"You don't want to quit us, Eddie, do you?" Schaffer rubbed his face.

"A vacation, a vacation," he pleaded. "Not quit. Just a vacation."

The mob conferred.

"That's different," they said. "We misunderstood you." They sent Eddie to Miami, but somebody constantly watched him. After two weeks he received a note. "You got enough sunburn, Eddie. Drag it back. Fast."

Sixteen months passed. Schaffer was now up to his $80 a week, and unhappier than ever. Again he asked to leave, and they called him into the lobby of the club where nine guys pushed him around until he sank to the floor.

"You're gonna stay, Eddie," said the spokesman.

The following week they relented somewhat, and gave Eddie a new car to drive. When they presented it, they rapped the windshield with a hammer. "See Eddie?" they grinned. "Bullet-proof. Ain't you happy now?"

Schaffer tried a booking agent, who had contacts with an opposition mob in Harlem. "I can get you in a Broadway show as soon as I get a release," said the agent.

A spokesman from the Harlem mob spoke to Lepke's bunch. "Eddie gets only one release," was the answer. "We release the body."

That night Schaffer told a few jokes that laid eggs. One of the boys came up on the stage. "You tryin' to louse up the show, Eddie?"

Schaffer wailed that eggy gags could happen to the best. "Okay, but don't lay 'em, Eddie," he was warned. Schaffer nodded. He had gone down from 186 pounds to 141.

He wasn't able to break his contract until Murder, Inc., disintegrated.

The club closed, the boys disappeared. Eddie came to work that night. The lights were out. The word was around that Murder, Inc., was in the hands of the district attorney.

Schaffer drew a deep breath and walked home.

I met him when he was working at Kitty Davis' Airliner, in Miami. He still wore the hot diamond ring.

"I'm pretty sure I know the guy who owned it," said Eddie. "But, it would be hard to return it. I'd have to go down to the bottom of the ocean, off Sheepshead Bay, and open a cement box. The guy is resting in there. But I don't think he wants the ring any more!"

One of the first assignments, I had when I went to work for the New York *Telegram* in 1923 was to cover the six day bike races in the old Madison Square Garden. The "six day night" held an endless fascination. The racing strings of riders in their variegated jerseys, the speed, the falls, the cheering crowd, stirred me, a Johnny Come Lately out of the Quaker City.

In the early morning hours the Garden became head-quarters for the most dangerous characters in New York. They came with pockets full of money and harlots decked in diamonds, for these were lush prohibition days, and only honest people were broke.

It must have been five o'clock one morning, when I left the press-box and stretched out in one of the spectator seats. Action had ended. Tired riders pedaled slowly around the pine track. The few remaining customers were dozing.

A bulky man, in expensive clothes, dropped into the seat beside me. He was drunk, but quite polite.

"You Jack Kofoed?" he asked.

I admitted such was the case.

"I like the stuff you write in the papersh. You got any enemiesh in thish town?"

"Not one," I said. "Not an enemy in the world."

He fixed me with a hard, but slightly wavering, stare.

"No kiddin'. You're my pal. Anybody you don't like, I'll knock him off, and it won't cost you a cent."

I assured him that there was not a person in the world who was not my blood brother. Then I went back to the press-box, and asked Hype Igoe who the drunk was.

Igoe looked.

"That," he said, "is Big Frenchy, the toughest guy in the Owney Madden mob. If you believe all the stories you hear about him, he's killed more men than the entire Marine Corps!"

That was my first meeting with a gangster. Sometime later "Mad Dog" Vincent Coll kidnapped Big Frenchy and forced Madden to disgorge $50,000 for his release. By this act Coll signed his own death warrant. He was filletted with tommy-gun bullets while making a telephone call in a drug store.

In succeeding years I met most of the notorious hoodlums who now and then claimed the headlines. It was impossible to avoid them. They owned the speakeasies and night clubs, and were to be seen at Madison Square Garden on fight nights. During horse racing months they piled into Miami, and many of the rackets were under their control.

Al Capone owned a house on Palm Island, which was the last word in over-done opulence. It was cluttered with expensive furniture. There was a swimming pool in the best Hollywood tradition. I went to one party there because I wanted to see the reputed king of the Criminal Empire in his gaudy habitat.

From a purely material point of view, it should have been a perfect party. Capone supplied unlimited champagne and Scotch from his personal hoard. There were turkeys and ham and caviar, and almost any delectable viand that could be imagined. But it wasn't fun.

The host, his greasy skin shining with sweat, looked on complacently, but his guests were ill at ease. Gunmen, arrayed in white flannels, white shirts and black suspenders, served food and drink. Their pistols, in shoulder holsters and hip pockets, did nothing to ease the tension. Because it was a hot night, the men had discarded their coats, so the artillery was clearly visible. They followed the guests wherever they went, even accompanying the girls to the door of the johnny, and waiting until the flustered damsels reappeared.

This was the night of the "St. Valentine's Massacre," when seven men . . . all of them enemies of the Capone regime . . . were lined against a wall in a Chicago garage, and mowed down by machine guns. If Scarface experienced any emotional reactions over that episode he did not display it.

After the party, though, he flew into a tremendous rage. His wife's diamond clip had disappeared, and he blamed the loss on the guests.

"If I find out who lifted that," he roared, "they'll never find enough of him to bury!"

Fortunately, before Scarface found it necessary to begin retaliatory action against those he had entertained, Mrs. Capone discovered that she had mislaid the bauble.

Like most of the gang lords, this man was not an interesting personality. He had little humor and an exaggerated ego. Few of my illegal acquaintances possessed more than a rudimentary education, or excited intellectual interest.

"Machine Gun Jack" McGurn, as ruthless a rodman as ever shot an enemy in the back, could be seen daily at the Bayshore golf course. One sunny morning he was playing there when Sheriff D. C. Coleman appeared with a warrant for his arrest.

McGurn came to the tenth tee flushed with enthusiasm, because he had played the first nine holes in thirty-three.

"I'll have to take you in, Jack," said the sheriff.

"Be a good guy," said McGurn. "This is the first chance I've ever had to bust seventy. Let me play the back nine."

"Not a chance."

"Look," begged McGurn, "frisk me. I ain't rodded up. You can go around with me. Honest to God, tinplate, I don't care about bein' arrested. It's happened a thousand times. Just let me finish the round."

But Coleman wouldn't listen to the impassioned plea, and no one ever found out if "Machine Gun Jack" could break seventy.

I did learn, years later, when gang wars had become only memories, that this killer was mowed down with the weapon that had given him his nickname.

It was an appropriate ending . . . and one that came to many who thought themselves above the law and decency.

VIII. THE MAN IN THE CROWD

Interesting personality has nothing to do with wealth or position. It comes from an inner flame.

VIII. THE MAN IN THE CROWD

THERE ARE MANY people in the world who are utterly unimportant, except to themselves, their families and friends. They are the Caspar Milquetoasts and

Joe Doakes of the world, the average man or woman getting on a crowded bus. Their hands make not only the deadly implements of war, but the gracious luxuries of peace. They cook and wait on tables, build houses and drive trains. Though they are the public, the public never knows their names. When they die, they are seldom listed on the obituary page, and never make the front page unless their endings are dramatic or tragic.

Yet, out of these people, who would be the last to proclaim themselves interesting, stem exciting stories.

There were John Henry Robinson and Bill Riddle, as examples. John was a middle-aged reporter for a San Francisco newspaper. A tidy, precise man, always dependable. Bill was a sportswriter on the same paper, also verging on middle age, but an unsatiable practical joker. They were very good friends.

John Robinson was married to a woman who was convinced of his constant infidelity. The fact that he worked all day and spent every evening at home, did nothing to swerve the lady from her absurd conclusion. She strafed him with accusations. She nagged him every day of his life. But John was a patient man, and loved her in his strange myoptic way. Eventually the nagging became as much a part of his life as three meals a day.

Bill Riddle, being a bachelor and something of a misogynist, was unable to comprehend such an attitude. It irritated him that his friend should be compelled to endure such an existence.

One day, John Henry Robinson went out of town on

an assignment that took several days. He returned, shabby and unshaved, after an all night ride on an "accommodation" train that was noted for its dirt and soot. He parked his luggage in the city room, and went to the nearest barber shop.

The idea for a gorgeous practical joke blossomed in Bill's mind. Among the innocent belongings in John's suitcase, he placed a brassiere, a pair of stepins, and sundry other articles.

Robinson returned from the tonsorial parlor, gathered his belongings, and took them home. He had a clear conscience. He was, in fact, a husband of impeccable virtue and very much in love with his wife, a fact which later events made clear. So he left the bag for his spouse to unpack, and returned to the office.

This jealous woman, in all her years of married life, had never found proof of her husband's infidelity. Now, as she unpacked the bag and lifted out the unmentionables placed there by Bill Riddle, she was sure that, at last, she had. The unfounded jealousies of those barren years became fact.

Mrs. Robinson flung on her hat and coat. She would go to the newspaper office, and before all his co-workers, expose John for a lecher. Hell hath no fury, they say . . . and for fifteen years this woman had felt herself scorned, innocent of evil though her husband was. In a blind rage, she rushed into the street.

A taxi, careening madly about its business, killed her instantly.

John was finishing the story to which he had been assigned when the police telephoned and told him of the tragedy. He completed the last paragraph, wrote '30' . . . and sent it to the copy desk. There was a pistol in his bottom drawer, momento of a murder he had covered. He went into the men's room and blew out his brains.

It was Bill Riddle, of course, who found the body.

That must have been fifteen years ago. Riddle, for all his joking propensities, was a friendly, easy-going man. He had no enemies. He disliked no one. John Henry Robinson had been his best friend. The tragedy shocked him as nothing in all his life had ever done. He went to the nearest saloon, and drank himself into oblivion.

That might also have been the immediate reaction of any other man, but Riddle did not stop there. He lost all interest in his work. He was concerned only in trying to forget the ghastly tragedy of which he was the author. The only way he could forget was to keep soddenly drunk. He, who had always found so much fun in life, became the most miserable of men.

There was only one end to that. He lost his job, and the succession of jobs that followed. The last time I saw him was on a winter day in New York. Riddle sat huddled on a bench in Union Square. He was a dirty, unshaved Bowery bum. His mind was as broken as his body. He seemed to recognize me in a vague, off-hand sort of way, and, as he babbled on, continually referred to himself as a murderer.

I offered to buy him a bottle of whisky, but he didn't want that. Good liquor had no more effect on him than water. Riddle, like the most wretched of his Bowery com-patriots, boiled down canned heat, and that vile concoction was the only thing that could warm and stimulate him.

I gave Bill five dollars, and went sorrowfully on my way. There was nothing to do for him, nothing in this world. He was beyond help . . . all because of a practical joke. He wasn't important, and he had no family, and no one seemed to care very much about him.

It was different with old Dad, though he had no one either.

Dad was a caddie at the Bayshore golf course. His badge bore the number "1" and he deserved it, for he had been tramping those lush fairways for two decades.

Dad's back was bowed, and his legs were crooked with the weight of years. His hair was white, but his mustache was browned by the chewing tobacco he always cuddled in his cheek.

Caddies, as a rule, are rough and ready young men who stand up for their rights. But they waived those rights for 82-year-old Dad. Caddies usually get a "loop" in the order of their appearance, but Dad was always first out no matter what time he appeared. The old man had a sort of counter-feit nimbleness. He looked as though he were hurrying, but he didn't go very fast, really.

Until he was nearly eighty, Dad did his two rounds a day, which meant trudging close to ten miles, carrying a heavy bag filled with iron and wooden clubs. But then he began failing a little. One loop was enough, and he came up the last fairway like a marathon runner, drooping with weariness.

He never asked for the best of it. He could not follow the flight of a ball as he once could, but was fiercely insistent that he could see as well as ever. The other caddies helped, though not obviously, so his feelings would not be hurt. They strolled to where they knew the ball lay, and stood around until Dad came up and saw it himself.

He had a strong pride, though he lived on no more than ten or twelve dollars a week. His name was Hugh Noud, or Dowd, or something like that, though I never heard it around Bayshore. He was Dad to everybody.

Perhaps he came from a fine old family; maybe he was a drifter from the wrong side of the tracks. But his pride was fiercely a part of him. Several seasons back a wealthy man, who had known the old caddie for a long while, wanted to put him in a home and pay all his expenses.

Dad's tobacco stained mustache bristled, but his voice was gentle as he answered: "I'm close onto eighty, and in all these years I've made my own living. I've never taken anything from anyone, and it is too late to start now. You are kind, and I'm obliged, but I'll stick it out this way."

He did stick it out, though his strength filtered away, and the bag he toted seemed to grow heavier every morning. There was the perfect example of what we are pleased to call the rugged American spirit. If Dad had to go hungry once in a while, and forego his tobacco occasionally, he preferred that to accepting anyone's help. And, though he was a little man in the comprehensive doings of the world, he was a strong man, worth more than he had been able to wangle out of a tight-fisted world.

He lived in a cheap little room somewhere, but Bayshore was his home, and the caddie shed his particular abiding place. He was lost anywhere else. Dad didn't feel sorry for himself. After all these years, the sight of the palms and the feel of the sun on his rounded back were as enjoyable as when he first came to the course more than twenty years before.

The old man caddied for me only a month before he died. His face was the color of a pine knot, but his hands were trembly, and his eyes were dimmed. So he passed away, and the boys in the caddie shed at Bayshore whispered, "Dad kicked off," and everyone was sorry and missed his presence.

He wasn't important. There will be no tombstone to mark his last resting place. But he symbolized something, the old man did. He symbolized courage and pride and self-sufficiency. He took nothing for which he could not return equal value. Materially, he might have been a failure, but he was a success in his soul. God grant him green fairways to walk upon, now that the tumult of the world is behind!

It isn't often, in wartime, that chaplains are given the credit that is due them. They are quiet men, not inclined to project themselves into the limelight. They are generally overlooked, and seldom mentioned. In one sense, they may seem to lack importance. I can't say that was true of Father Tom Sherry.

He was chaplain of the 102nd Infantry in the first World War. He went to the front with his boys. He heard their confessions and gave them absolution when they were dying.

Father Tom was a great guy. Priest or not, he was regular and could be touched for a few francs. He was Irish, which explains a lot of things. When his regiment was ready to go into action, he hitched a holster containing a .45 automatic to his belt.

"Of course," he said, "I am a man of God, and a non-combatant, but the Jerries don't always take time to look at the Roman collar. Sometimes they get nasty with a bayonet, and I don't think the good Lord would object to any man protecting himself."

Actually, Father Tom didn't care so much for himself. The doughboys were his sheep, and some of them didn't have much time to live. The priest wanted to herd them to heavenly pastures, but he also wanted to ease the misery of their days on earth. Being an infantryman at the front is the hardest and filthiest of all existences.

The 102nd went to Fere en Tardenoise. It was rough going. When the road is hard a soldier needs tobacco. In 1918 the boys used Bull Durham and rolled their own when they were behind the lines; they saved the tailor mades for ugly hours. It's hard to roll a cigaret when your hands are trembling, and the machine guns sound like a million typewriters printing "Death" in capital letters.

When the 102nd arrived at Fere en Tardenoise there wasn't a pack of cigarets in the outfit. Logistics were not handled as well than as in the second World War.

Father Tom knew about the lack of cigarets. He knew all the inner, tear-drenched secrets of the regiment, and there was no secret about the lack of tobacco. He couldn't let them go into combat that way. Imagine being hit, and the attack streaming past; no telling when in hell the stretcher-bearers would get to you, and no fag to puff on.

There was only one place Father Tom could think of where he might get some. Sixteen miles back was a rest area which boasted a canteen. The day was hot, and the roads were dusty, but the priest took a barracks bag, and began to walk. At a good, steady pace, it takes four hours each way for a trip like that. Dust-grimed and sweaty, he finally arrived at his objective.

"Cigarets?" said the fat noncom in the canteen. "Sure we got 'em, Father. Plenty." He laid a pack on the counter. "One to a man. That's the rule."

The priest said patiently. "My outfit is in the lines. They're going over tonight. Maybe you don't know what that means. I do. They haven't any cigarets. I want all I can carry back to them."

The other shook his head.

"One pack," he repeated. "That's the rule. There ain't no use arguin'. One pack."

Father Tom was not a young man, and he was tired. He might have seen the commissary officer, and run into the same argument. So he simply unholstered his automatic.

"Sixteen miles I've walked," he said. "Sixteen dusty miles, and I'm not going back with one pack of cigarets. I have money enough here for one hundred cartons, and it is one hundred cartons I am taking back with me. It would be too bad if this gun of mine went off. Both you and I would be very unhappy about it. Here is the money. Count off one hundred cartons into that bag of mine, and be as quick as you can about it, my son. I still have sixteen miles to walk before I get back to my regiment."

The sergeant looked into the priest's steady blue eyes, and then began piling the cigarets into the barracks bag.

Father Tom walked those sixteen dusty miles back to Fere en Tardenoise, and the 102nd had cigarets when they attacked at dawn. Though he was a man of God, he was a realist, with love in his heart, and iron in his soul. Father Tom was killed in the Argonne, and he isn't remembered by anyone but those members of the 102nd Infantry who are still alive.

IX. COLUMNS I HAVE WRITTEN

To Jack Kofoed, Jr.,
and his comrades . . .

IX. COLUMNS I HAVE WRITTEN

IN A MANNER of speaking, good columns
—or rather, the better ones—write themselves. They are
felt so strongly, that emotion is translated to paper without

the struggle demanded by less heartfelt ones. Writing something means feeling it first; feeling it deeply.

One Saturday evening, before the end of the war, I returned home after a broadcast. As I came into the hall I heard my wife sobbing. No one had to tell me what had happened. I knew. Our oldest boy, who was on Okinawa with the Sixth Marines, had been killed. The fatal telegram had arrived. Uncounted fathers and mothers know the stunning impact of that shock; how the blood turns to water, and the knees to sand.

Hours later I sat down to do my Monday stint. The business of living does not cease because so much has gone out of life. There was only one thing in my mind and heart —my son who had been so strong and handsome. Somehow, writing about him was an emotional release:

"Casualty lists are merely sad, impersonal columns of names until that of a loved one appears on it. Then, it wraps up in one line of type all the sadness and futility of life . . . all the beastly terror of war.

"Our boy . . . Corp. Jack Kofoed . . . of the United States Marines . . . was killed at Okinawa. Big, six foot, three inch Jack, with his blond hair and blue eyes. Not quite twenty years old. A wife with whom he had spent only a few weeks; a baby he had never seen.

"Now, he's gone. The fate that rules humanity must have a bitterly cynical sense of humor. Our youngest and finest thrown into the hopper to die or be mutilated. Every city in the world crawling with the useless and unfit; profiteers, slimy black market operators, playboys. It doesn't augur well for the postwar world everyone talks about, if it is to be shaped by such as they.

"I felt sad when Mr. Roosevelt died. That sadness was intensified when Ernie Pyle was killed, for I had known and admired him. But it is different now. There is a numbness inside . . . a sort of unbelieving wonder. Roosevelt had risen to one of the great places of history. Pyle had lived life to the full for 40-odd years. But Jack . . . like John S. Knight's boy, and thousands of others like him . . . had not even begun to live. All the gay and eventful and successful years were ahead. Now he will never know them.

"All that is left are a picture on the living room wall and a cross on a stinking Pacific Island.

"The kid went out because he was an idealist. He joined the Marines when he was only seventeen. 'From the halls of Montezuma to the shores of Tripoli.' They fought everywhere. They were given the toughest assignments. That's what Jack asked for.

"After his boot training, and commando training, and all that sort of thing, they sent him to a V-12 course at Bucknell University. It would last a couple of years, and he would get a commission. After a little while the boy rebelled. I was serving on the staff of Lt. Gen. Carl A. Spaatz, commanding general of the United States Strategic Air Forces in England. Jack wrote me that he had joined the Marines to fight, not to go to school. He wanted out.

"What argument could I give him? Wars are won by the men who fight. America has lived because of such men. But my heart was cold when I told him to go ahead and follow his conscience. I had seen two wars. I had seen men die. So Jack transferred to the 29th Marines, of the Sixth Marine Division . . . and when the invasion of Okinawa started I knew that was it. All parents who have boys at the front know that feeling.

"There may be no mail for weeks on end, but as long as the telegram does not come, there is hope . . . painful, worried hope; but hope just the same.

"Then . . . with that single piece of paper . . . the world crashes upon your ears, as it has crashed about the ears of millions in the past sad five years. We may win great victories on land and sea, but to parents like us, whose sons have paid the price of those victories, flavor has gone out of the news. We are as staunchly American as ever; as determined to do all we can to help, but there is something different.

"Lord! When you look back. That sunny September morning in 1939. Remember Neville Chamberlain's sad and tired voice on the radio, announcing that Great Britain had declared war on Germany over the invasion of Poland? It was dramatic, but very far away.

"We didn't know it, but to thousands of parents those words were the death sentences of their boys, who were still in grammar school and high school.

"I don't want to be maudlin. Life, in its entirety, is more sweat and tears than laughter. Things happen and if you are to retain sanity, and carry on the business of living, you must accept tragedy as you accept joy. If there is a living God, as ministers and priests tell us, there will be a reward for Jack's eagerness and honesty and courage. We must all die sooner or later, and his passing was brave and gallant, though it came too soon.

"But, why should it be? Why should the people of the world still live by the law of claw and fang? I think of Jack, because Jack was ours . . . but it is as true of every other boy who makes up the millions of dead. They didn't want mud and cold and danger; the heat of the tropics, endless weariness, bombs and shells and bayonets. All they wanted was a chance to live and love and work. That chance was never given them.

"I never saw my boy in uniform. Our last meeting was quite casual. Jack was joining the Marines, and I drove him to Marion's house . . . she is the girl who became his wife, and the mother of his child. We shook hands and said a few words.

"All I remember saying was 'It's going to be tough, son. Do your best and don't quit.'

" 'Okay, dad,' he answered grinning.

"There was nothing to indicate that this would be the last time I would ever see the boy I loved so much. If there had been . . . Well, I don't know. There was nothing more that could have been said, nothing more in all the world.

"All we have now are memories . . . inconsequential, lovely memories. I remember how he looked a few hours after he had been born . . . the first day he went to school . . . how I'd cuddle him on my lap, and sing songs of the last war in a gravelly voice . . . the night he went, handsome and solemn in cap and gown, to get his diploma at Edison High.

"No, I don't want to be maudlin, but those things come back and fill my heart. Jack did his duty as he saw it, and now there is nothing left but the picture on the wall and the cross on Okinawa."

That column was written from the bitterness of a heavy heart. Bitterness died, though sorrow remained. I had a letter from Jack's company commander, Captain Howard L. Mabie, of D company.

He wrote: "There was no finer non-commissioned officer in the regiment. Everyone liked Jack. He was hit at night, and half a dozen men risked their lives to get him back to safety. The day before that happened he came to me and told me that his daughter, Karen, had been born. I have never seen a prouder or happier man."

The heart-break of that! The great joy that could not last even twenty-four hours! I wonder, when he was hit by that bastard Japanese that got him, whether or not he knew he would never again see the girl he loved, or his baby.

When I was a little fellow death seemed a terrible thing. I was afraid of it. The Dark Angel came to our neighborhood—to my grandmother; to old Mrs. Schmitt, the cobbler's wife; to a man who was knocked down by a trolley car on Germantown Avenue; to Mrs. Cummings, who was burned to death one winter morning when she tried to hurry the fire by putting kerosene oil in the stove.

In the passing years I saw the Angel come in many

forms: to a quiet bed in a quiet room; in automobile and train accidents; in bombings and strafings. Now, death no longer wears a frightening mein. The Angel brings a gift. None of us knows what that gift is . . . but I am sure it is a good one.

What lies beyond that River Styx is shrouded from our eyes. Having seen, for too many years, man's inhumanity to man, it is not hard to believe that what faces Charon's passengers must be better than what this world offers.

Not that I have any regrets about my life. It has been full and interesting, with no monotony to dull its days. It has had joy and sorrow, and some small measure of accomplishment.

I have been frightened under bombing and shelling, as millions of others have been, but I thought: "If it gets me, I hope it's quick." It is not death, but pain or mutilation that frightens us. Death is the peace that follows battle.

In other days I doubted a future existence. Since our boy died with his gallant Marine comrades at Okinawa, I doubt no longer. Those boys were fine. They had too many potentialities to be rubbed out like chalk marks on a slate.

Those potentialities will have a chance to develop in a kinder life than we have here. It's got to be that way. Life would be completely futile, otherwise. Death must be the gateway to something better.

Believing this, one must develop tolerance toward his fellows, even though they are of different races and religious beliefs. All the writing and preaching in the world cannot bring tolerance. It comes only of suffering and understanding. But . . .

"A man is a man, no matter what his race or color or religion. In spite of all the high talk of freedom and democracy and the bright new world of tomorrow, we are still bound with the thongs of bigotry and narrowness. Protestant and Catholic and Jew and Negro lives within the boundaries of his color or faith. Each may be an American, but he isn't entirely an American, because his breed and religion are things apart from other Americans.

"He becomes defensive. He spotlights the virtues of his own kind, and damns the faults of others who are different. Human nature being what it is, that's probably the way it always will be.

"Not long ago I wrote of Jews who were heroes of this war, and of the last one, too. Some protests reached my desk. These said 'the God damned kikes won't fight, and never would fight.'

"Of course, the history of war proves that courage is part of every racial heritage. No breed or color is without it. I've been under fire of bombs and shells and small arms, and I know how it feels. Your guts crawl. Your mouth dries up. You're hoping that, if anyone is hit, it will be someone else. Everybody feels that way. The hero is the guy who doesn't let it get him down.

"The doughboy in Germany knew that while his Nazi foe was brutal, he wasn't yellow. The Marines and dogfaces in the Pacific know how much courage the Japanese they burned out of caves and dugouts possessed. That's why I had a bitter laugh at the few who told me the Jew wouldn't fight.

"Don't say that to Field Marshal Sir Bernard Montgomery, who has neither illusions nor sentiment. He might tell you about Maj. Felix Laibman, and the mine field at Mechili.

"In the summer of 1942, Germany had the world in the palm of her hand. All the Desert Rat, Rommel, had to do was finish Montgomery, and the super-Axis strategy for a juncture with Japan could be completed.

"The holding of the mine field did not win the war. It was a vital factor, though, in a touch-and-go moment. A company of Jewish engineers from Tel-Aviv went out to lay the mines. They were bombed by Stukas. They were hemmed in by tanks and infantry. Five hundred went originally. For two weeks . . . part of the time without food, part of the time without water . . . they held out in the stifling heat.

"The force was reduced to ninety, five of whom went raving mad. The air reeked with the smell of rotting human flesh. Rifles became so hot they burned palms and fingers. The Stukas never stopped coming over. These were Jews, remember, the men who wouldn't fight. Then, at last, they were saved by a French flying column under Gen. Koenig.

"A Jewish soldier took down the blue and white flag of Zion, and rolled it up. Gen. Koenig asked him why.

" 'We are not permitted to fly that flag, sir,' answered

Maj. Laibman, who had commanded the engineers from the start.

" 'Pardon,' said Koenig. *'Je m'em fous mal des regulations'* (which in a rough translation is: 'I don't give a damn for regulations!') 'That flag goes on my car next to the tricolor.'

"I don't care about a Jew as a Jew, or a Protestant as a Protestant, or a Catholic as a Catholic. To me such words are labels. Each man or woman stands on his or her own feet. I've known guys with a million bucks and degrees from Harvard who didn't shape up as well under fire as the tough kid who didn't get by the sixth grade in Public School 98.

"If humanity could learn tolerance and respect for the other fellow, this would be a pretty good world to live in. If any good ever came out of the war, it is the understanding that develops between men who face death together.

"The funny part of it is this: We are all going to die. Nobody ever escaped it. The only difference is that death may come to soldiers in the next sixty seconds, and it may come to the civilian in the next sixty years. It is that inevitable. Yet in spite of this fact . . . in spite of the fact that death makes no distinction of race or creed, we continue to think of ourselves as so much better than others.

"York . . . Smith . . . Doolittle . . . Cohen . . . Donaldson . . . Delly . . . Laibman . . . Courage is as common as fear. Understanding is as rare as tolerance."

I have always felt a great distrust of diplomats and world

statesmen who control the lives and destinies of lesser men. The San Francisco conference gave me a hook on which to hang that distrust:

"Anthony Eden gave a dinner to Edward Stettinius, Molotov and Dr. Soong in the early days of the San Francisco conference. They are diplomats; the top layer of diplomats. Diplomacy, as we know it, has brought the world to the edge of ruin. It has killed millions. I don't trust diplomacy.

"I've sat in poker games and tried to make people believe the deuces I held were three aces. But I was playing with dollars. The big shots play with lives. In the business of diplomacy you can be an outright liar and have blood and murder and arson on your hands, as many of the Axis foreign experts had, but you may still wear striped trousers, a top hat and an air of unshakable dignity.

"The four men at the dinner party were very important. They represented Winston Churchill, Harry Truman, Josef Stalin and Chiang Kai-shek. These men run the world now that Mussolini lies in a morgue, with his face a spittled pulp. Hitler is gone from the scene, and Hirohito is an errand boy instead of an emperor.

"When I was a boy, the names of Washington and Lincoln and Napoleon seemed unapproachable. But the men who wore them were human beings like the rest of us. They had the same faults and passions and sorrows. This is true of everyone.

"That must have been a grand dinner party at San Francisco. Martinis to start with. I don't like martinis, but

Eden and Stettinius and Molotov and Soong apparently do. Then they had oysters and sirloin steak, peas and asparagus, and ice cream, with crushed strawberries.

"At the same time, dirty doughboys and Marines on Okinawa were nibbling on dried boxed rations, if they had time to do even that.

"Afterwards the diplomats lit cigarets, and discussed details that will decide what will happen to you and me, and your child, and the boy of mine who is left.

"When they were through, they returned to their suites, donned pajamas and went to bed. When they arose in the morning they had to go through the matutinal chores all of us have to do, and chances are that, under the shower, minus the top hats and striped pants, they didn't look like rulers of the world.

"If they could . . . with all their power and training and sophistication . . . get around to one sentence uttered by a completely humble Jewish carpenter: 'Do unto others as you would have them do unto you,' there would be no more wars and no more international troubles.

"But they won't. They never will. I'm not a smart guy. I never built a big business. I don't know anything about the science of government. But I do know millions of fine people have been slaughtered because men in striped trousers, who settle our destinies over martinis and steaks, do everything but get down to fundamentals. There is only one: 'Do unto others . . .'

"But nobody ever does.

"Victor Herbert once wrote an unforgettable song. Part

of the lyric goes, 'And, love and love alone shall rule the world.' He wrote that because he was an Irishman, and sentimental. Sentiment hasn't any place, except with us little people. We *are* little. What have we got to do with the events in San Francisco? Nothing.

"If all the mothers and fathers in the world suddenly banded together and said to the big shots: 'You get cold and hungry and sick and drunk just as the common man does. You're stronger and wealthier, but you don't know any more about the fundamentals of life than we do. Either settle the peace of the world or we'll give you what the Italians gave Mussolini' . . . what do you think would happen?

"There was a lot of talk about the meeting in mid-Atlantic, when the Atlantic Charter was written, and more about Teheran and Yalta. Unless enduring peace comes out of those meetings, they might as well have been arranged by a Hollywood movie director. Words can be magic weapons, or they can be blunted swords. This isn't a movie script. The life or death of civilization hangs in the balance.

"The church tells us God has left our destinies in our own hands. The drunken bums in front of Madison Square Garden, to whom I used to dole out quarters on Friday nights, could not order their lives. We, as a race, have not been able to order ours.

"Wilson, Clemenceau, Lloyd George and Orlando didn't do so well in the Hall of Mirrors in Versailles. What will Stettinius, Molotov, Eden and Soong do over their martinis and steaks in San Francisco?

"Maybe I have become cynical. Millions of fathers and mothers all over the world have become cynical, too. I'm sick of brilliant sophistries and promises. I've listened to them mouthed by everyone from city councilmen to prime ministers, and they were all cut from the same cloth. It is easy to talk, less easy to perform.

"All I know is that I've got my belly full of destruction and violent death. The men in the striped pants, who dine in state, have tried every trick in the bag except the one they know nothing about:

" 'Do unto others as you would have them do unto you.' "

Personal experiences, even minor ones, are often grist for the unsatiable mill of the daily column.

"I was in Philadelphia Saturday. It was nearly nine o'clock, and we were about to get down to the serious business of contract, when I decided to run the car in the garage before the—should I say ice-cream soda?—had a too dizzying effect.

"In the rear of the house is a driveway that extends the length of the block, and is as dark as a Scotchman's pocket. I had just put the bus away, dutifully turned out the lights and started to enter the house by the back door when there was a spurt of flame . . . the crack of a pistol shot!

"Immediately upon its heels came the fusillade, a half dozen guns opening up at once. It was like a raiding party caught by the enemy, trying to fight its way back to the safety of its own lines.

"I cocked my head around the corner of the garage, curiosity getting the better of a natural antipathy toward bullets . . . A man came toward me, running with a limping jerk, since he had been hit in the leg . . . Once he turned to shoot at the men pursuing him. Then he went on.

"At the other end of the drive a policeman was lurking, pistol in hand . . . The fugitive must have guessed it . . . He was trapped, hemmed in with death . . . I wonder what desperate thoughts sped through his mind? . . . Afterward they said he was a three-time loser, and this rap would mean at least twenty years in a steel cage.

"The watch-dogs of the law were clamoring at his heels . . . The cop in front of him stepped out of the shadows and said: 'Stick 'em up!' The thief didn't stick 'em up . . . He fired . . . Missed . . . The patrolman shot him point-blank . . . The thief coughed and turned blindly to his left down the cross-drive.

"The firing suddenly stopped . . . I just heard the pad of feet on the cement . . . Hoarse breathing . . . Then they caught up with him . . . He fought like a cornered wharf rat . . . There wasn't any chance for him to get away . . . and he knew it . . . But he fought, anyway . . . for a moment.

"There was a street lamp close by. I had followed on the heels of the pursuers, and in the thin, yellow light saw the end of the little drama . . . The man's face was turned toward me . . . It was a strong, good-looking face, but the lips were writhed back from the teeth and the eyes were those of a badgered wildcat . . . He had been shot in the chest . . . There was a blackened hole in the front of his shirt . . . The blood from a wound in his arm had run down and smeared his hand as he lifted it to defend himself.

"The picture lasted only for an instant . . . Then the police were at him like flies around a syrup-can . . . There were panted oaths and groans and the sound of blackjacks on a human skull . . . Then the little knot of struggling men fell apart . . . The thief lay unconscious on the cement . . . He looked as though he were dying . . . It didn't seem reasonable to believe he could last very long . . . He breathed with a high, reedy sound, like a broken whistle.

"The uniformed men talked excitedly . . . Their voices trembled a little . . . The district detective rapidly frisked the man they had finished . . . and found little enough . . . No loot save a string of crystal beads that wasn't worth $10 . . . A life for a string of beads . . . Looked like a bad exchange.

"Windows went up . . . Neighbors called to each other . . . Raw, elemental little drama was unprecedented in that quiet neighborhood . . . They came out timidly and gathered around.

"The policeman who had fired the last shot kept saying, 'The lousy bum, suppose he had hit me. What would my three kids have done?' None of the others expressed themselves about the man who seemed to be dying at their feet . . . They crowded close with morbid curiosity and tried to get a look at his face . . . Just another casualty in the war between Society and the criminal . . . 'Good enough for him . . . He might have got into my house . . . or mine . . . or mine . . . Don't forget to lock all the doors and windows tonight, Harry . . . Lord, people aren't safe in their own homes any more.'

"A gong clanged in the street . . . The ambulance! . . . The thief was rolled onto a stretcher and lifted into it . . . The detectives and the uniformed men, except for the patrolman on the beat, climbed in after him.

"Bong, Bong!

"The ambulance roared off into the darkness.

"The bluecoat on the beat developed a sudden new importance . . . Before this he had been a slightly flat-footed man edging along into middle age, good enough to walk up and down the streets and see that school children crossed the trolley tracks on Ogontz Avenue in safety . . . Now he was a soldier who had been under fire . . . He had a notch on his gun . . . or would have when the thief died.

"He kept on telling people how some one had seen the man enter one of the homes, and had telephoned to the station . . . How police were stationed at each end of the drive and in front of the house, and how the fellow had walked out the back way with a gun in his hand . . . and fired the instant the detective challenged him . . . His chest swelled a little . . . He was immensely pleased with himself . . . And rightly enough, too, since he had carried himself so well in unexpected action.

"The neighbors clustered around, staring awe-struck at the blood on the cement . . . But one by one they drifted away . . . Silence again fell over the driveway . . . Our foursome went back into the house . . . Our host mixed drinks.

"We sat down at the bridge table . . . There were shaded lamps, a grand piano in the corner, and the soft inflection of women's voices . . . Four spades . . . doubled . . . Ease and quiet . . . And I thought of the manhunt in the driveway, and the cracking guns, and the blackjacks . . . and the broken body stretched out on the cement, and the cop who wondered what would have happened to his three children had he gone down . . . It takes that sort of thing to buy ease and quiet for the rest of us . . . Your lead, dear!"

X. MUM'S THE WORD

The stories you don't see about important people. Headliners with their hair down.

X. MUM'S THE WORD

IT IS A newspaper axiom that the best stories are those that cannot be written, and there are columns that ache to be written, and never are. Some never will be.

A few appear disguised as chapters in a novel or in other, less inhibited, corners than a daily newspaper stint.

I might have written one about a publicized woman evangelist, who appeared in New York a good many years ago. The city editor sent me to Boswell her doings in the Manhattan night. It can be said for the lady that, while she was God's chosen daughter in the pulpit and in her interviews, she was something less than that in her off hours.

The evangelist paraded the night spots from eight until closing, which in those days was any hour you might care to name. Some of the joints she visited were noted for the filth of their comedians' repartee and the nudity of their chorus girls. Mrs. Diety had a whale of a time. She was supposed to be drinking nothing but ginger ale. There was ginger ale in her glass, but it was belted with rye or bourbon until her eyes grew slightly glazed and her coiffure mussed.

The jokes made her laugh, though some were stomach-turners, even for the habitual attendants at such places. Her interest in the unclothed bodies of the youthful hoofers indicated a slight leaning toward Lesbianism.

It was about five in the morning when Mrs. Diety decided that, for the moment, she had had enough of New York night life. I'll say for madame that she could hold her liquor and was reasonably sober. The remaining members of the press, who were trailing her, asked if there wasn't something on which she could be quoted.

"Of course," she said. "I have seen tonight the evils

which imperil the young people of New York. I have seen them in many of these places, dancing over the pit of hell. Oh, that I could save them! Oh, that I could call them to the gentle arms of Jesus! Why are such places as these night clubs permitted to exist?"

She finished the liquor in her glass and rubbed beautifully manicured fingers across her forehead.

"Christ!" she exclaimed, "I'd better remember to take some aspirin before I go to bed, or I'll feel like the hinges of hell in the morning."

Such conversation is not unusual in night spots, but coming from one who proclaimed herself the chosen daughter of God, it was something of a shock. Mrs. Diety was lush and curved, and stirred something more than thoughts of religion in the minds of the male sex. But I don't like hypocrisy, no matter whom the practitioner may be. I would have loved to paint an honest picture of her. But what good would it do? The lady had converted many people. Thousands of others looked on her as a feminine Messiah in shining robes. Why shatter their faith in her, when that faith was something big in their lives? Besides, the editor would have blue pencilled the yarn, if I had written it.

There might have been another column about a very nice chap, who was big enough in many ways to be headline bait. He was rich and important, and suffered from perpetual skirt trouble. Beautiful women kept him in the stratosphere of ecstasy or in the swamp of despondency.

It was necessary for Borton Bartholomew to make frequent trips to London in the interest of the huge industrial firm of which he was an executive. Nothing was ever said in the home office about a fair-haired English girl, who lived in a ground-floor apartment in the exclusive West End Grosvenor Street neighborhood. As a matter of fact, because Mr. Bartholomew was extremely circumspect, the home office knew nothing of this lady.

Borton Bartholomew was a sophisticate. His tastes were transient, and he did not expect too much constancy from the women he temporarily adored. But . . . being a married man with a Westchester environment . . . he was inclined to keep his peccadilloes to himself.

The gentleman arrived in London on a cold, foggy February day. He had announced his coming in advance by cable, so everything was prepared. This, of course, was pre-war, when yellow lights shimmered through the fog, and cases of Scotch were easy to get.

Bartholomew's inamorata greeted him with the sweet-face formula that is as sure fire in the backwoods of Georgia as in the flats of London. They were tremulous in the Olympian hills when a knock sounded on the door. It was an imperious rap . . . the rap of a man who was used to that flat. The lovers relaxed their amorous clasp upon each other.

"I thought," said the lady, "that Horace was out of town. You must hide until I can get rid of him."

Borton Bartholomew was in the embarrassing position of being as unclothed as Adam before he sank his teeth into the apple. Ecstatic as he could become over a blond, it was important there be no scandal.

"What do I do?" he whispered.

"Hide in the closet," his sweetface told him. So, Mr. Bartholomew, fumbling through the dark, opened a door, and closed it softly behind him. Not being oriented to this new flat, he had opened the door to the street, and found himself in the fog and cold of an early February morning!

Fortunately the London bobby, underpaid and overworked as he is, possesses a depth of understanding. One of them found Borton Bartholomew. He first wrapped the unhappy executive in his raincoat, asked the minimum questions, found a night-hawk taxi and sent Mr. Bartholomew to his hotel . . . the Savoy or the Dorchester, no doubt.

But what point would there be in exposing Borton Bartholomew to the gibes of others?

I had no such inhibition about Battling Siki, but I didn't write the story when it was new because the managing editor thought it indelicate.

Siki was a Senegalese; a man of magnificent physique, slashed and scarred by bayonet wounds. He won the light heavyweight boxing championship by knocking out the Gorgeous Orchid, Georges Carpentier, in Paris. This was a mistake. It had been arranged for Carpentier to win, but the Senegalese, angered by an unexpected hard blow, struck out viciously, and the ageing, handsome Frenchman collapsed. But Siki was stupid enough to defend his title against Mike McTigne, at Dublin on St. Patrick's Day, and not unreasonably, lost the decision.

He came to America with a fanfare of publicity, this much decorated black war hero with a blond Dutch wife. The little brains with which he had originally been endowed were addled by what he had endured at the front. New York's boxing fans knew nothing of such terms as psycho-neuroses. They simply described Siki as "punch drunk" or "slap happy," which was sufficiently descriptive.

Having lived on the ten sous a day of a Senegalese private, the comparatively fabulous amounts he received for fighting in the ring upset Siki completely. He visited West Side speakeasies, and ordered drinks for everyone. When the bill was presented, he either gave the bartender a hundred dollar bill, or wrecked the place and beat up half the customers — depending on his frame of mind. When the generous mood was on him, he filled his pockets with dollar bills and, with a pet monkey on his shoulder, went forth to give away the money.

Siki's manager, a fat and tired man named Bob Levy, seldom had a complete night of sleep. Almost invariably, at three or four in the morning, the police called and said: "We've got that crackpot fighter of yours again. Shall we keep him until morning, or do you want him now?"

In spite of his drinking and sexual excesses, of which he was peacock proud, the Senegalese fought well enough to earn a match with heavy-fisted Paul Berlenbach, the light heavyweight champion of the world. Though he felt it was almost hopeless, Levy tried to impress on Siki the importance of getting into condition, and winning the fight.

"It's worth a million dollars if you beat Berlenbach," Bob reiterated day after day. "A million. Think of it!"

The Battler nodded vigorously, and flashed his amazingly white teeth into a smile. Sure. He understood. A million. Apparently he did, for the brothels and speakeasies of Hell's Kitchen knew him not at all during those days of training. When he climbed into the ring his belly was ridged like a washboard; he was hard, bone hard, and his black skin shone like polished ebony.

Siki needed perfect condition, for Berlenbach was the most murderous hitter of his time. But, as it turned out, the Senegalese did not fight. He protected himself sluggishly and ineffectively and made few offensive moves. The bout turned into a slaughter. Paul's gloves grew soggy with the blood of his enemy. The black flesh was torn with knife-like blows. Siki reeled and staggered under the barrage, but punishment did not stir him out of his lethargy. At last the referee sickened of the massacre, stopped the fight, and awarded the victory to the white man.

Levy had a car waiting in 49th Street. After his wounds had been patched and he had showered, Siki climbed sullenly into the automobile and sat down beside his wife.

"I can't understand it, Bat," said Bob Levy. "Maybe Paul was too good for you. Maybe you couldn't beat him any time. *But you didn't fight!* That's what I can't understand. *You didn't fight!* You just took it. And you never did that before in all your life. Why?"

The Senegalese growled deep in his throat.

"It's her fault," he said. "You say I make meelion dollar if I win. This afternoon she call me black son of a bitch, and say she want a white man! I no make meelion dollar for theese women, Monsieur Levy . . . not if Berlenbach keel me! That's why I no fight!"

This, it seems to me, was the most extraordinary alibi for defeat ever advanced by anyone. Battling Siki never had another opportunity to make a million for his Dutch blond, or for anyone else. Not long after that fight, he was found in a Hell's Kitchen gutter with several bullets between his shoulder blades. The police did not solve that murder. Perhaps they were not too anxious to solve it. One of their perennial headaches had been removed, and it might seem ungracious to arrest the man who had supplied the aspirin.

There was another couple I didn't write about, either, because they bore well-known and distinguished names. Even now, of all the names concerned, the only real one that can be mentioned is that of the bartender in the story, "Mother" Kelly. Kelly later graduated to ownership of a highly successful place of his own.

"Mother," in spite of his feminine nickname, is a bulky Irishman. He gained his accolade while working for the fabulous Texas Guinan. It was bestowed because he was unfailingly sympathetic to those suffering from crying jags and to chorus girls whose boys had done them wrong.

Kelly was working in one of the Swing Lane bistros . . . and a fellow sees a lot of what is called life when he mixes drinks behind a 52nd Street bar. The intrigues of men and women come startlingly into the open under the influence of alcohol.

Anyway, the woman in this story was a blond called Lola, who had a figure no one could pass without noticing. The man was like a thousand others you see on Wall Street or Park Avenue: well dressed, quiet of manner. He answered to the name of Jim.

Mother Kelly had seen the woman often before . . . but not with this man. She had dropped in frequently with a tall, raffish fellow. They sat at a table, held hands, and each presumably told the other that he was the most remarkable person in the whole world.

It isn't any part of a bartender's business to inquire into the history of his customers, but nobody can prevent him from wondering what's going on. From scattered words that reached him, Kelly began to get a picture of the eternal triangle. Lola and Jim were married. Then she had fallen for a matador in sheep's clothing — the fellow she had sat with so often in the bistro.

"I didn't really love him, Jim," the woman said. "He just fascinated me. He was so . . . so different from anyone else I had ever known. You were never able to say the things he said so easily . . . and probably didn't mean at all. But it's over now . . . It's honestly over. I'll never see Manuel again."

At that moment Mother Kelly looked past them, and saw Manuel standing behind the two. The drink mixer's first impulse was to duck behind the bar. Frustrated sweethearts are often quick with gun play, and a stray bartender or two never matters to them. But Manuel wasn't reaching for a weapon. He had a package in his hands, and he held onto it tightly while he talked.

"You can't do this to me, Lola," he said. "I'm mad about you . . . utterly insane. You told me you were through with your husband. This thing must be straightened out once and for all. He can't want you after the way you have treated him."

"I do want her," said Jim. "And I've heard enough from you, anyway. Get out of here!"

Kelly reached under the bar for the pacifier . . . a blackjack of which Detective Johnny Broderick would have been proud. If trouble started, he was ready for it.

Manuel's voice softened from the almost hysterical pitch it had reached.

"I've brought a bundle of letters here," he said. "After you've read them, Jim, maybe you won't feel the way you do now. If you're a real man you won't." He laid the bundle on the bar. "I'll be back in an hour to see what you say." He turned abruptly and left the place. Mother drew a breath of relief. He'd have the cop on the beat in here an hour from now . . . just in case . . .

Lola said in a still sort of voice: "That wasn't like him, Jim. I thought he would come in shooting. These letters . . . I want you to read them . . . I haven't written anything I'm ashamed of."

Jim picked up the bundle with one hand, hooked the other through his wife's elbow. "Let's take a little walk,"

he said. Mother drew a breath of relief and said to himself:
"I hope they don't come back!"

An hour later Manuel returned, disheveled, distraught,
his eyes like holes burned in a blanket.

"Where are they?" he demanded.

The bartender shook his head. "You've got me, brother.
They took that bundle of yours and went for a walk."

Manuel drew a deep breath. He leaned across the bar
and whispered, "By this time they're both dead . . .
blown to bits. That package was a bomb." He began to
rave. There was nothing for Kelly to do but call a cop
and have the guy arrested. An alarm was sent out for
Lola and Jim. Maybe the infernal machine had not ex-
ploded yet. Maybe there was a chance for them to live
and salvage their love.

It was close to four o'clock in the morning when the
couple walked into the bistro. Kelly let out a yelp that
could be heard at Columbus Circle.

"The package . . . where's the package?"

"You mean the letters?" Jim asked, knowing the bartender could not have helped hearing what had occurred.
"We took a taxi to Central Park, and then walked . . .
talking things over. I made up my mind there was only
one thing to do . . . start all over again . . . wipe out the
past completely; so I threw the letters into the lake without
opening them. From now on we're going to be happy!"

Mother Kelly relaxed. "I guess that calls for one on the
house," he said. "It's the first time I ever heard of a husband's generosity saving two lives. What will you have?"

XI. UNDER FIRE

Little people in the midst of
war react peculiarly. A few
become heroic without knowing it.

XI. UNDER FIRE

THE PUBLIC RELATIONS offices of the Army, Navy, and Air Force in the European Theatre of Operations, occupied 28 Grosvenor Square, London W.1. This had been one of the most "posh" neighborhoods in the British capital in peace-times. Only those with wealth and social position occupied houses or flats in Grosvenor Square, and adjacent streets such as Curzon and Davies.

Each afternoon at five o'clock, a brigade of charwomen came in to clean. It mattered not to them that activity continued. On hands and knees, they scrubbed and swabbed, and only a moment later countless tracks streaked across the wet floor. But, with true English apathy, they went about their business.

One of the women was named Mrs. McElratty. She was an untidy person, with fat legs encased in shapeless cotton stockings, heavy, sagging breasts and whispy hair. Somehow, Mrs. McElratty always seemed wetter and dirtier than any of the other charwomen. She had acid on her tongue whenever she became angry. One might comb the world, but he'd find no woman less likely to play the part of a heroine. Still, Mrs. McElratty was a heroine, even though such a thought never occurred to her. If anyone had mentioned this fact, she would probably have said in her coarse voice, "You're bloody well pullin' my leg, ayn't you?"

Robot bombs began to strike London a week after the Allied troops made landings on Omaha and Utah beaches. Day and night were filled with the jeep-like sound of motors, and the tearing crash of tons of explosives. London became a front line, as it had been in 1940. Thousands of homes were destroyed; thousands of men, women and children killed or mutilated.

Yet, no matter how bad the day had been, the charwomen came to 28 Grosvenor Square to scrub the floors. Mrs. McElratty was numbered among them only three times a week. Those were the hours when her husband, a member of a heavy rescue squad, was assigned to night duty. The rest of the time she insisted on being home to make dinner for " 'er 'Arry" when he had finished his labors. It was just as well, for Mrs. McElratty had varicose veins, and, I suspect, a touch of asthma. The work was difficult for her.

She and her husband lived in a frame house in the poverty-ridden East End. One afternoon a buzz bomb hit their street, sheared off the front of their residence, and left little of the house except the kitchen. The blast hurled Mrs. McElratty across that kitchen, and one side of her body was bruised from neck to heels. Considering that many of her neighbors had died, this was too minor to bring complaint. An hour later she took her market basket, and went to the fishmonger's to buy a bloater or haddock for supper. Women were already queued. Though Mrs. McElratty was stiff and sore, and her varicosed legs gave her trouble, she waited her turn.

When she had her fish, she started back for what was left of her home. Again her luck saved her. Another bomb struck the fishmonger's shop, killing him and his line of customers. Though Mrs. McElratty was two blocks away, she was knocked down again, and this time a bone in her left wrist was cracked. But she held on to her basket of haddock and limped into the wreckage of her home. Out came the pots and pans, and soon the odor of fish and chips filled the air.

Mrs. McElratty told me about this when she returned to work next day. It never occurred to her that she had done anything unusual. She was proud that she was better off than her neighbors. By putting scantlings and tarpaper over the front of the house, she and her man had a place to sleep. After all, the kitchen had not been harmed, and the kitchen was the most important room.

"But the dinner," I said. "It seems to me you would have been too battered and nervous to bother with that."

"Bother, is it?" She laughed her high pitched, unpleasant sort of laugh. "You don't know my man, 'Arry. When 'Arry comes 'ome from work, 'e wants 'is dinner, no matter what 'appens. War or no war, bombs or no bombs, 'Arry 'as got to eat. Them Germans ayn't stopped me from gettin' 'Arry's dinner yet. And, they won't unless they drop one of the buzzers right on me 'ead!"

Britain's recognized heroes of the European war are Montgomery's desert rats of the Eighth Army, and the bombers and fighters of the Royal Air Force. No one will recognize Mrs. McElratty's right to be among them, but that is where she belongs. Hollywood would never cast her as a heroine, but she is as typical of the soul of Britain during the war as the silver-tongued Churchill, himself.

While she scrunched on her knees, wielding the brush with her right hand—she still couldn't use her left—Mrs. McElratty's thin hair worked loose from its fastenings.

She smelled of soap and sweat, and her bloomers sagged under the edge of her skirt—but she was England just the same.

All sorts of heroes came to Grosvenor Square before D-Day . . . Lt. Col. Francis Gabreski, who shot down more Germans than any other fighter in the Eighth Air Force; Sgt. Maynard Smith, our first enlisted man to win the Congressional Medal of Honor; yes, even Lt. Gen. Jimmy Doolittle. But of them all, my favorite was Flight Officer — later Second Lieutenant — John C. Morgan.

Red Morgan was a husky young man, quiet and unassuming. Probably one of the reasons was that he was a co-pilot. Unless something happens to the man in the left hand seat, the co-pilot is a fifth wheel on the wagon. In combat there is nothing for him to do but talk to the gunners over the inter-com system: "Hey, ball turret, there's a Focke-Wulf coming in at six o'clock . . . Top turret, get the dust out of your eyes, and look at that ME109 buzzing you at twelve o'clock." That's all, and in the newsstories the only mention of him comes at the bottom, such as: "Second Lieutenant Wysocki was the co-pilot." Men have developed inferiority complexes on less than that.

Of course, when there are enough casualties, co-pilots get ships of their own, and become as cocky as those from whom they have taken orders.

One dawn, Morgan's bomber took off on one of the worst missions any air crew ever had. The flak was bad as they crossed the German coast, and a sizable piece of steel sheared off the back of the pilot's skull. He was a big man, a strong man with enormous vitality, and he did not die at once. In his delirium he thought he was flying the ship, and fought the controls. Morgan, holding him off as best he could with one hand, kept the bomber in formation. He would have called for help, but flak had ruined the inter-com. There was no way to tell the crew of his plight.

They were still two hours from the target, and five until they might hope to set their wheels on the hard strip of the home field. It requires skill and strength to fly a B17 in formation. Flying it under the conditions that faced Flight Officer Morgan is unthinkable. A less brave and determined man would have pulled out of formation and turned back. Red thought of the explosives in the bomb bay and the targets for which they were destined, and kept on toward Germany.

In the meantime, the rest of the crew were experiencing their own particular brand of hell. The flak was not only heavy and accurate, but the Luftwaffe sent swarms of their best fighters against the attacking bomber squadrons. In they came, machine guns chattering, while the big ships ploughed steadily onward.

The top turret gunner of Morgan's ship was a quiet man named Sgt. Tyre Weaver. As he manned his weapon, a shell sliced off his left arm at the shoulder. Pouring blood, but still conscious, Weaver stumbled down from the turret. Lt. Keith Koske, the navigator, tried to give him first aid, but the arm was torn off so close to the shoulder that it was impossible to use a tourniquet. Koske sprinkled the wound with sulfa powder and gave Weaver an injection of morphine, but that was all he could do. The gunner would bleed to death long before they arrived at the base.

The navigator was a sensitive boy. He died a thousand deaths during every mission. As he looked into Weaver's shocked eyes, it suddenly came to him what he must do. It was a million to one shot — nothing less — but if he didn't take it, Weaver would die.

"Look," he said, sounding calm and confident, though his nerves were raw, "I'm going to toss you out. You'll get picked up and taken to a hospital."

"No," whispered Weaver desperately. "No. You can't do that to me, lieutenant."

Koske didn't argue. He couldn't. If he did he'd break down and scream. He couldn't take much more of this. He felt himself going to pieces. While Weaver watched, he opened the escape hatch, and the updraft caught the sergeant's pilot chute and made it billow out.

"Believe me, it's the only way," said Keith in a choked voice. Suddenly he shoved the man through the hatch. He watched until the parachute opened, then he sat down, with his head in his hands, trying to hold himself together. He mustn't think. He must keep busy . . . Weaver had been such a good fellow . . . What a lie to even pretend he would live to reach earth and be hospitalized! Stop thinking, God damn it! Stop thinking! Do something. He climbed into the top turret, and manned the guns. They were splattered with Weaver's blood.

While this drama was being enacted, Flight Officer Morgan flew the bomber toward its destination. The pilot had not died yet, but his struggles were growing weaker. Red was almost exhausted. Every muscle ached. His mind was hazy with exertion and horror. The compartment was like a slaughter house, with its welter of blood.

He made the bomb run, cut away and joined formation for the run back home. Then the bombardier came in.

"Thank God!" Morgan whispered. "Take him away."

The pilot was carried to the bomb-bay and given first aid, but died a few minutes after his ship's nose pointed toward England. It was still rough going, for the fighters, bitter at having failed to break up the bomber squadrons, kept attacking. Finally they were over deep water and the green fields of England were in sight.

Flares were fired to tell the ground crews that dead and wounded were aboard. Flight Officer Morgan set his battered plane on the runway to end the most terrible of all his aerial trips.

John Morgan was presented the Congressional Medal and promoted to second lieutenant for what he had done.

But Morgan, with his own plane to pilot now, wanted action. He went out a couple of times more, and then was shot down.

The amazing thing, though, was that Sergeant Weaver actually landed in Germany and was picked up before he bled to death. The million to one deal worked and instead of dying, Weaver spent months in a prison camp, and came out alive.

I must tell you about Snuffy Smith. Snuffy was a thin little man, who wouldn't have been picked as a hero any more than Mrs. McElratty would be selected as a heroine. After he was recommended for the Medal of Honor, he was taken off operations. The Eighth Air Force wanted men who had won America's highest honor to be alive when it was presented. The way the ack-ack and the Luftwaffe fighters were operating, Sergeant Smith might be another posthumous case before he could be decorated.

Secretary of War Henry L. Stimson was in England on an inspection trip. Everyone was happy to have the secretary make the presentation in person. But Smith, wearied of the monotony of the base, went AWOL several times, and the squadron commander put him on kitchen police.

When Stimson arrived, along with the full brass of the Eighth Air Force, Snuffy Smith was peeling potatoes and washing pans. Fifteen minutes before the ceremony he ripped off fatigue clothes and donned his class A uniform. The medal was presented . . . and when the show was over, Smith returned to his kitchen chores.

The army is realistic. You may be a hero, but you must obey orders or take the consequences. A year or so later, Snuffy Smith appeared at the redistribution center at Miami Beach. By this time the stripes had been peeled from his arm and he was an ordinary buck private.

Privates are a dime a dozen, but Smith had something

those other privates probably never would have, the Congressional Medal of Honor. He not only wore the ribbon, he pinned the bit of metal on his chest, so no one could mistake it.

One afternoon, while strolling Lincoln Road, he was spotted by a couple of military policemen, who had never heard of Sergeant Maynard Smith. Not unnaturally, they believed him to be a phony, and placed him under arrest. Snuffy said nothing, for he was riding pretty and knew it. When they arrived at the guardhouse and the matter was unravelled, two flushed and sweating M.P.'s tried to laugh off the matter.

One of the few heroes who looked the part, as the movies portray it, was a fighter pilot named Major Walker Mahurin. He was handsome and modest, and just what the casting director ordered. On the other hand, one of our top aces was a wild kid, who had been the town bad boy and still was when it came to shooting down Germans. But all those eagles were outdistanced by Lt. Col. Francis Gabreski, a Polish boy from the Pennsylvania coal regions, who had a nose reminiscent of Jimmy Durante's.

Those fighter aces finally came to regard their "kills" as a ball player does his batting average. Gabreski, having broken the record, was ordered home. He dropped into Grosvenor Square for a chat, and was very happy about the whole thing. The left side of his blouse was covered with ribbons. He knew he'd have a terrific time when he was again with his family and friends.

There were a couple of days to wait and Gabreski found them monotonous. He decided to make one more mission. It was probably all right, but the more superstitious members of his group tried to talk him out of it. Gabreski said it was all nonsense, and those silver leaves on his shoulders carried a lot of weight.

At eight o'clock that night we received word that Lt. Col. Francis Gabreski was missing. It seems we'd get used to that sort of thing, but we never did. My cousin, Lt. Glen Kofoed, came to see me only two days before he went on his last mission. Death is always close.

It didn't turn out as tragically as all that, so far as Gabreski was concerned. We learned the next day from his wingman that a motor was shot out. The day was bright and clear, and they were over the German airfield they had strafed. The young colonel knew he couldn't get home, so he brought his plane down smoothly on the Jerry's hard strip. His wingman circled around and saw his chief climb out of the plane, hands up. Being a prisoner wasn't good, but it was better than being killed. Gabreski was released when the dogfaces of the infantry finished German resistance.

In World War One there wasn't much bombing. The boys went out in their box kites and dropped sticks of dynamite. Those things could kill you awfully dead if they happened to land on you, but the odds were in your favor. However, when a thousand planes, each carrying several thousand pounds of demolition or fire bombs went out, that was another matter.

I often wondered what it would be like to go on a bombing mission. During the day I saw the sky filled with our Fortresses and Liberators. At night, for hours at a stretch, I heard the thunder of Royal Air Force bombers going over. There was something soothing in the sound, for I knew we were dishing it out.

In the 1914 war I saw something of artillery fire and machine guns, but this was different. This was something the world had known nothing about until the Big Show started. Of course, all over London could be seen what the blitz of 1940 had done, particularly in the East End and the City. But there's a difference in seeing burned out remains . . . and going through what burned them out.

It was in February, 1944, that the Luftwaffe began throwing what was left of their Sunday punch. Lt. Col. Donald Wilkens and I were sharing a flat in a three hundred year old building in Shepherd's Market.

The Jerrys got through a couple of hundred bombers each night. That doesn't sound like much compared with a couple of thousand, but they can do a tremendous amount of damage. Don and I put on our tin hats and went up on the roof to watch the show. We kept under what cover there was. What goes up must come down, and ack-ack guns threw up tons of steel.

The show was beautiful . . . like every Fourth of July fireworks display put together in one great exhibit. Flares the German bombers dropped to mark their targets . . .

tracer bullets arching up at them . . . anti-aircraft shells . . . occasionally a plane exploding in mid-air. The symphony of hatred beat upon the eardrums continually. The guns whanged without interruption, punctuated by the thunder of rocket guns in Hyde Park; the blast of bombs accompanied by sheet lightning effect.

It would have been thrilling to watch, except for that one thought of what would happen if one of those bombs dropped close by.

The Germans were methodical. Every night at exactly ten minutes after eleven the "alert" sounded and a little later the bombers were overhead. At ten minutes past twelve the "all clear" sounded. The National Fire Service tried to quench flames while the heavy rescue squads dug mangled men, women and children out of the blazing wreckage.

One night as Wilkens and I watched from the roof, a dozen flares stopped directly overhead. I don't think I'm more of a coward than the average man, but I said, "I don't like it. That's an aiming point. There never was a squadron without a bombardier who couldn't get excited enough to drop one in the wrong place. If he does, we're in for it . . ." Then a big one hit in St. James Square, not far away, and I thought our rattletrap building would collapse with shock.

At twelve-ten they went away. The night was cold and damp. As I climbed into bed and pulled the blankets up to my chin, I told myself that when the sirens sounded tomorrow night I was going to the shelter. Bombs can't be argued with. Anyone who doesn't get concrete between himself and them, is nothing but a fool.

However, at one-ten the Jerries came back. At the siren's first scream I reached for my clothes, but the air was so cold I pulled my arm back under the covers. "When the first bomb falls, I'll go," I promised myself, but inertia conquered fear. For the duration of the little blitz, neither Wilkens nor I took shelter. Not that we were brave — it was just too much trouble.

I am interested in the psychology of heroes since I'm not one myself. Phonies will tell you they aren't scared. The medal winners admit they are.

One of our greatest fighter pilots of the war said that his brain bunched up like actual muscles on the top of his skull as soon as he went into combat. There never was time to figure out what to do. The winner did the right thing instinctively. The man who was killed was the one who stopped to think. That's why I think heroism hasn't much to do with what is commonly called courage. It is often a matter of reflexes. A person does something instinctively, it's right, and he lives . . . and the other fellow doesn't. This makes me think of a fellow named Fred McKay.

Fred was a big, handsome Canadian heavyweight prize-fighter, who had the look of a champion, but he wasn't a champion. Though he could box and hit, he seemed to lack courage. When the going got rough, McKay quit. It finally became so bad that no promoter would sign him.

When the first World War burst upon a startled world, McKay returned to Canada where he enlisted in the infantry. Eventually he became a company commander. He won a dozen medals and citations for courage above and beyond the call of duty . . . and then he was killed. The fight fans thought McKay was as yellow as a canary's wing. His men never knew a more courageous leader. It's hard to estimate courage before it is put to the test.

While sitting in the corner of a ring waiting for the gong to sound Fred had time to worry about what the other fighter might do to him. He tightened. He was unable to relax. But when bullets and shell splinters, instead of fists, were flying, he managed to do the right thing. McKay died leading a desperate counter-attack . . . this big, good-looking man, who had quit time after time in the ring. Those things are hard to understand, but they happen every day in wartime.

Perhaps because my ancestors were Scandanavians, I was unusually interested in the Nazi invasions of Norway and Denmark. Those nations were no match for the Nazi war machines. Besides, since Norway was betrayed by Quisling and Sundlo, much of the resistance that might have been waged was paralyzed at the start.

On the highway from Trondheim to Storlien stood a little fort called Hegre. Its commandant had sold out, as Quisling had done. When the Germans appeared, he ordered immediate surrender. His second in command was a lieutenant. The boy's country had been invaded and he understood only one answer to that: to fight as long as breath remained. When the captain ordered his men to stack arms, the lieutenant answered with the Norwegian equivalent of "Nuts!"

Surrender? Surrender when men and guns and ammunition were at hand? Why had they been trained and armed? War had come to them uninvited, and by all the gods, they would fight for Norway!

The shavetail unholstered his automatic.

"Captain," he said, "I don't like to call harsh names, or make accusations, but this looks like treason to me. We're going to hold this fort as long as we can." He turned his hard glance on the soldiers. "I'll shoot the first man who leaves here. I'm willing to die for Norway, and I expect you to feel the same."

The soldiers were with him. The common man usually sees his duty and does it. Probably because nobody thinks of buying him off. They manned their weapons, and the Germans, who had expected to walk in unopposed, found themselves in a tough fight.

The unhappy commanding officer was in a quandary. There was no way for him to carry out the treasonable bargain he had made. But he had one small revenge. He ordered the lieutenant to the post that was under the heaviest fire. That was where the subaltern would have gone, anyway, for he was that kind of man. He was killed there. The Nazis smashed through and took Hegre and the few remaining soldiers. They did one more thing. They killed the commandant because they thought he had betrayed them, and that was justice of a rough kind.

War is filth and sorrow, destruction and death, the crucifixion of mankind on the cross of his own building. But it does highlight the courage, honesty and humaness of such people as Mrs. McElratty, Flight Officer Morgan and the little lieutenant at Hegre.

Out of the first World War came a letter that has become a classic; a letter which might have been written by any father about to go into battle. It was penned by Major Frank Cavanaugh, a strong, gentle, kindly man, who became famous as a football coach at Fordham University. Much as he loved Davie, the boy to whom this letter was written, he treated him just as he treated other candidates, when Dave tried for the Fordham eleven.

He wrote:

"Dear Davie boy: Your good mother writes me that you have a chum who lives next door, and she says he is a fine boy. I wish I had a chum. You and your mother used to be my chums, and sometimes Joe and Billy, and even dear little Rose Marie, and Phil, too, when he was home. But, now, all that is changed, and I have no chum in all the world. I think it is rather sad sometimes, don't you? But, I have your picture, which I take down sometimes, and talk to when I'm lonely.

"Didn't we have great times together, and wasn't it fun when you'd come to the car to meet me? Then, when you saw me getting off, do you remember how you'd hide behind a tree, and run up behind me, and scare me after

I had passed? And, do you remember how you and I would race, and you were getting so fast you'd beat me sometimes, for you were getting to be a great big boy.

"And, then, we'd all go down to see the circus, and the parade, and hold hands so we wouldn't get lost. And, then, Christmas! Oh, wasn't that a wonderful day? Early in the morning we'd rush downstairs to see our presents, and then poor, tired mother would work and work to give all you boys a Christmas dinner . . . turkey, cranberry sauce, plum pudding and candy and nuts and everything.

"Oh, Davie, did any little boy ever have a mother such as yours? I wonder. And, now you are to have another Christmas, and Cav won't be there. But I want you to have the finest time you ever had on that day, so I may be happy over here, thinking of you. I wish I knew some little boys and girls here, so I could talk to them, and hold their hands, and I would call them by my boys' and girls' names, and pretend I was home.

"The other night I had a wonderful dream, and I was so disappointed when I awoke. I dreamed I was sitting in our kitchen with mother and David and all the children, and the chair which was tilted against the wall, slipped and fell gently, without hurting me, to the floor. Mother and you, and all the children, laughed and laughed, like good, naughty people. And, you came over, and took my hand, and lifted me up easily.

"Isn't that funny, Dave? Think of my little boy lifting a big, fat father from the floor with one hand! Then, we laughed some more, and suddenly I remembered it was

161

after nine o'clock. I said: 'Why, what are you children doing out of bed this time of night?'

"And, you said: 'It isn't often our father goes away to war, so we thought we'd stay up and say good-bye.'

"Then, I was so surprised to learn that I hadn't gone away to war yet that I suddenly awoke to find myself in my lonely barracks, with the rain coming down hard outside, and I was lonesome for my dear family.

"Now, David, old boy, everybody is in bed but me, trying to get lots of health and strength for the big fights we shall soon be in, so I must do likewise, and end this letter to you.

"You must remember that your father came into this great war for the sake of all little children, and I know you will, while I am gone, take good care of mother and the children. I can see you growing up, tall and straight, with shoulders back and head up, because that's what old Cav wants, and you love Cav, don't you, Davie boy? Will you do something real nice for me? Will you kiss mother and Annie and Billy, Rose Marie and John for Cav, and send one to Philip in Maine?

"Excuse me, Davie, for writing in pencil, but ink is hard to get. The lights are going out in a few minutes, so good night, good-bye, Dave, and God bless you. From your old man,

Cav."

That letter is a summing up of men at war. More bitter than weariness and pain and death is loneliness. There isn't anything worse. Just loneliness.

XII. CALL IT

'30'

Summing up. The leg
man stops legging it
around the world.

163

XII. CALL IT "30"

PHILADELPHIA . . . New York . . . Chicago
. . . London . . . Paris . . . now Miami. It's beautiful here
and it's warm and peaceful. There's none of the tumult of

Broadway or the Grandes Boulevards or Piccadilly Circus. People seem to sluff off some of their arrogance when they come to Miami.

It seems a little funny to think back to Germantown Avenue as I stroll up Flagler Street or Biscayne Boulevard. Then I was in awe of the people who caught my attention . . . of "Silent John" Titus, Florence Lawrence and the few like them; even now people hold a fascination for me.

There is a lot of difference between the neighborhood in which I was reared, with its little dull buildings and uneventful days and Miami with its clean, bright, modern constructions and crowded hours. There is even more of a difference between the scrawny kid who stood on the Huntingdon Street bridge and the man who finally did what he set out to do — meet interesting people.

At first, back in Philadelphia, I admired from afar. I touched but few and then, remotely. When I began my newspaper career, a new phase started. This meant pursuing the people I wanted to know . . . pinning them down with questions. Some aroused my admiration, others were disappointing. Many were shallow, egotistical and hard to know, but in general I found them genuine, gracious and friendly.

I shall never forget the first time I met Franklin Delano Roosevelt. I was writing a sports column for the New York *Journal*. When we were introduced, Mr. Roosevelt exclaimed, "Oh, *Jack Kofoed!*" as though I were someone important. The tone of his robust voice and the twinkle in his eye seemed to add, "Of course. I read everything you write." His knack of conveying such impressions was part of the man's charm; certainly one of the great contributing factors toward his success.

I remember Ambassador John G. Winant the night his son was reported shot down over Germany. He came to Col. Jock Whitney's flat at No. 1 Grosvenor Square, where we were having a staff meeting. Mr. Winant looks remarkably like Abraham Lincoln. That night, shadowed with sorrow, the resemblance was even more striking. He was reticent and said nothing of his loss. It wasn't until later that we found out about the grief he concealed that night.

I remember Dr. and Mrs. Wellington Koo, with whom I flew in a C47 from LaGuardia Field in New York to Prestwick, Scotland. He, the most brilliant of Chinese diplomats, and she, the sister of Madame Chiang Kai-shek. They were continually delightful, as gracious to mechanics as to generals.

But now, in Miami, life is better than it has ever been . . . or so it seems. There is a greater ease in living. If I sound as though I have withdrawn from the crowd, with only nostalgic memories to keep me company, the conception is untrue. Miami is a world crossroad. It's just the place to do research on my hobby . . . people. And it's never hard to find material to fill my daily column for the Miami *Herald*.

Here I have met many show-world celebrities. Harry Richman, Sophie Tucker, Joe E. Lewis, Billy Vine, Larry and Mildred Schwab, Luba Malina, Phil Baker, Tony Martin, Joe Frisco. Golfers like Bobby Jones and Walter

Hagen; Willie MacFarlane and Byron Nelson. Ball players such as Bill Terry, Mel Ott and Rogers Hornsby. Prize-fighters in the upper brackets: Jack Dempsey, Bill Stribling, Jack Sharkey. Authors and columnists: Eustace L. Adams, Philip Wylie, Hervey Allen, Marjorie Stoneman Douglas, Walter Winchell and many others. They all come to Miami sooner or later.

A few haven't come this way yet. There are two in particular that I want to see here. Col. Ben Lyon, Jean Harlow's co-star in "Hell's Angels," and his lovely wife, Bebe Daniels, who is a star in her own right. I was a guest in their London home often and I'd like to return some of their hospitality. They rate high on my list of interesting people. And the list is long.

There must be an element of the unusual . . . a touch of inner excitement, perhaps . . . that makes people interesting. There is no end to the interesting people in Miami, just as there is no end to my interest in them.